LET ME GO TO THE FATHER'S HOUSE

LET ME GO TO THE FATHER'S HOUSE

John Paul II's Strength in Weakness

Stanislaw Dziwisz and Czeslaw Drazek, SJ

Renato Buzzonetti

Angelo Comastri

Pauline
BOOKS & MEDIA
Boston

Library of Congress Cataloging-in-Publication Data
Dziwisz, Stanislaw.
   [Lasciatemi andare : la forza nella debolezza. English]
   Let me go to the Father's house : John Paul II's strength in weakness
/ Stanislaw Dziwisz and Czeslaw Drazek ; Renato Buzzonetti, Angelo
Comastri. — 1st English ed.
      p. cm.
   ISBN 0-8198-4522-1 (pbk.)
   1. John Paul II, Pope, 1920–2005. 2. Suffering—Religious aspects—
Christianity. I. Title.
   BX1378.5.D9613 2006
   282.092—dc22
                                                2006019989

Cover design by Rosana Usselmann

Cover photo: *L'Osservatore Romano* Photo Service

Original edition published in Italian under the title *Lasciatemi Andare: La forza nella debolezza di Giovanni Paolo II*.

Copyright © 2006 Edizioni San Paolo, s.r.l. – Cinisello Balsamo (MI)

Translated by Matthew Sherry

First English edition, 2006

Published by Pauline Books & Media, 50 Saint Paul's Avenue, Boston, MA 02130-3491. www.pauline.org.

Printed in the U.S.A.

Pauline Books & Media is the publishing house of the Daughters of St. Paul, an international congregation of women religious serving the Church with the communications media.

1 2 3 4 5 6 7 8 9   11 10 09 08 07 06

CONTENTS

The Days of Suffering and Hope

Sainthood Now!

FOREWORD

BETWEEN THE END OF MARCH and the first days of April 2005, a breathless world followed John Paul II's suffering and passage to the Father. That this was a time of grace was clear to the crowds that came from all over the world, surmounting all sorts of difficulties to be at St. Peter's Square and then at the tomb of John Paul, whom they regarded as a man of God and called upon as a saint.

His suffering and tenacity were striking. Although the elderly pontiff could no longer speak, everyone understood that his death was the ultimate act of love offered to God on behalf of Christians, other believers, and all people. This book gives us the opportunity to relive that time of grace through the testimony of three eminent persons who were close to John Paul II for different reasons. The first part was written in collaboration by Father Czeslaw Drazek and His Eminence Cardinal Stanislaw Dziwisz, who for years was the pope's personal secretary, but above all his friend and confidant. This part recounts the Polish pope's great love for those who suffer, and the desire he showed from the first day of his pontificate to be close "to the sick, the poor, the suffering, the least fortunate." Karol Wojtyla was intimately familiar with suffering, having experienced it in his childhood and youth with the deaths of his mother, his brother, and his father.

Then came the dramatic years of Nazi war and persecution, followed by Soviet occupation and the dictatorship of the Communist party. All of these episodes made John Paul II "the pope of the sick and the suffering." On May 13, 1981, Ali Agca brought the pope, in Archbishop Dziwisz's words, "to the shrine of pain and suffering," where he had his most intense experience of closeness with those who suffer. The pontiff's Way of the Cross continued silently through the years until its consummation on April 2, 2005. And when he expressed his desire to go to the Father's house, it seemed natural to those standing nearby to sing, not the prayer for the deceased, but the *Te Deum,* the song of thanksgiving to God for the gift of the person of the Holy Father and his tremendous pontificate.

The testimony of his personal secretary is accompanied by that of Professor Renato Buzzonetti, the pope's personal physician since 1978. The doctor recalls the pope's many hospitalizations at the Gemelli, nicknamed "Vatican III,"[1] but also the attitude of profound interior serenity that led him to accept sickness, pain, and forced inactivity from the hand of God. This account also contains some previously unpublished details on the dramatic events of the assassination attempt and the pope's last days.

At the end, His Excellency Archbishop Angelo Comastri, who manages St. Peter's Basilica, describes the emotionally charged devotion of those who defied all discomfort to come to Rome for one last farewell to this great pontiff. Such devotion shows no sign of decreasing, because "the procession of faithful and devout crowds continues past his humble tomb dug into the earth of the Vatican hillside." And this isn't superstition! These people know that John Paul II was entirely dedicated to the service of God and of Jesus Christ. By paying homage to the pope, they praise the Lord who gave him to the Church and to our age.

Elio Guerriero

---

1. The Vatican itself is known as "Vatican I," and the pope's summer residence at Castel Gandolfo as "Vatican II" [trans.].

SUFFERING IN THE LIFE AND TEACHING OF JOHN PAUL II

by Stanislaw Dziwisz
Archbishop of Kraków

and Czeslaw Drazek, SJ
Editor of the Polish edition of
L'Osservatore Romano

THE DAY AFTER HIS ELECTION to the See of Peter, John Paul II manifested his desire that the apostolic service he had accepted in a spirit of obedience to Christ should become, "from this very moment, a ministry of love in all its manifestations and expressions."[2] This desire was continually realized before our eyes. One of the most characteristic features of the Holy Father's pastoral activity was his close connection with crowds, individuals, groups from various backgrounds, members of different religious faiths, and people from all walks of life. Among these, a privileged place was occupied by the sick, the poor, the suffering, the "least brethren" (Mt 25:40)—all

---

2. *Insegnamenti di Giovanni Paolo II*, vol. 1 (1978) (Vatican City: Libreria Editrice Vaticana, 1979), p. 16.

those deprived of their dignity and their fundamental rights.

In the Holy Father's teaching, man is the first and primary way of the Church, but this is especially true of suffering man. The most perfect example of the respect due to man is Jesus Christ, who, loving all, embraces with his greatest love those people who are sad and suffering.

This attitude of love shaped the pastoral style of John Paul II, a style described very well by Cardinal Joseph Ratzinger when, on October 16, 2003, in the name of the College of Cardinals, he presented Pope John Paul II with best wishes on the occasion of the twenty-fifth anniversary of his pontificate:

> Over these twenty-five years, you, as the Vicar of Jesus Christ in the apostolic succession, have tirelessly traveled the world, not only to bring beyond every geographical boundary the Gospel of the love of God, made flesh in Jesus Christ; you have also crossed the boundaries of the spirit, of those so often far from one another and opposed to each other, in order to bring the estranged together, make friends of those who are separated, and make room in the world for the peace of Christ (cf. Eph 2:17). You have addressed yourself to the young and the old, to the rich and the poor, to the powerful and the humble, and have always demonstrated—following the example of Jesus Christ—a special love for the poor and the defenseless, bringing to all a spark of the truth and love of God. You have proclaimed

God's will fearlessly, even where it is opposed to what people think and want. Like the Apostle Paul, you can say you have never sought any honor from men, but have cared for your children like a mother. Like Paul, you also are enamored of mankind and have desired to make them partake not only of the Gospel, but of your very life (cf. 1 Thess 2:5–8). You have taken upon yourself criticism and injury, but have roused gratitude and love and brought down the walls of hatred and estrangement. Today, we are able to witness how you have placed yourself entirely at the service of the Gospel, permitting yourself to be consumed (2 Cor 12:15). In your life, the word "cross" is not merely a word. You have let yourself be wounded by the cross in soul and body. And like Paul, you also bore suffering in order to make up in your earthly life, for the Body of Christ that is the Church, what is still lacking in the sufferings of Christ (Col 1:24).[3]

We would like to place a particular emphasis in these reflections on this dimension of the life and ministry of John Paul II, marked from the beginning by the stigma of suffering that he transformed into an instrument of apostolate.

Strength in Weakness

The cross accompanied John Paul II from the first years of his life. He was struck by the suffering that

---

3. *L'Osservatore Romano,* October 18, 2003, p. 8.

always leaves a deep and permanent mark on the human soul, because it comes from the premature loss of those dearest to one. At nine years of age Karol lost his mother; four years later his older brother, Edmund, passed away. Edmund was a doctor and died at the age of just twenty-six after catching scarlet fever from one of his patients. The young Karol's memory was deeply marked by the image of his father standing beside his son's casket, weeping and repeating the prayer, "Your will be done."

The experience of suffering in his earliest years found expression in the youthful poetry of Karol Wojtyla: *Upon Your White Tomb* and *Magnificat*.[4] In the first poem, the nineteen-year-old poet recalls his mother's premature death—"love extinguished"— and says with sadness: "Oh, how many years have passed without you, how many years?" On his mother's tomb, "the white flowers of life" bloom, and he, her son, bends down over her tomb to renew his prayers for her. In the second poem, inspired by the words of Mary's hymn, he glorifies God for the beauty of the world that surrounds him, for youth, for poetry, for joy and suffering.

After the death of his mother and brother, Karol remained alone with his father, but even this family tie gave way in February of 1941. Returning home

---

4. Karol Wojtyla, *Tutte le opere letterarie* (Milan: Bompiani, 2001), pp. 37, 39–43.

from work, he found his father dead. He was 62 years old.

At the beginning of Karol's second year at the clandestine major seminary in Kraków, another suffering struck the young man. On February 29, 1944, while he was returning from the Solvay factory where he worked as a laborer, he was hit by a German truck, which left him with two head wounds. Karol was brought to the surgical clinic, where he remained in recovery for two weeks. He was always grateful to the person who, after the accident, found him unconscious and saved his life.

His personal sufferings were united with those of the whole nation, which was going through the hard years of war and the terrible Nazi occupation. At the end of the conflict came the times of struggle against the imposition of the Communist system. In his book *Memory and Identity,* he recalls that "anyone who was inconvenient for the regime was persecuted: for example, the former combatants of 1939, the soldiers of the Polish National Army after the Second World War, the proponents of the intelligentsia who did not share Marxist or Nazi ideology. Normally this meant elimination in the physical sense, but sometimes it meant elimination in the moral sense: the person was more or less drastically prevented from exercising his rights."[5]

---

5. John Paul II, *Memoria e identità. Conversazioni a cavallo dei millenni* (Milan: Rizzoli, 2005), p. 22.

The years of his priestly and episcopal ministry coincided with a period of persecution against religious convictions, of struggle against God, of limitations on the Church's activity. But this pastor was always with his people, appealing on their behalf for a decent life. He dedicated special attention to persons oppressed by physical or spiritual suffering. At the very beginning of his pastoral ministry in the Archdiocese of Kraków, on the day of his entry into the cathedral on March 8, 1964, he wrote a long and cordial pastoral letter to the sick, telling each of them that he was "very close to you in my heart and in the spirit of faith," that he wanted to grow close to each one, because the sick occupy an especially important place in the Church.[6] He wrote similar letters to them over the following years, entrusting to the prayers and sacrifice of the sick the important intentions of the Church, the diocese, and the country.

In his parish visitations, he always went to meet with the isolated and the sick. He visited those who were bedridden at home, in hospitals, and in rest homes. His meetings with the suffering—as he himself affirmed—"deeply moved him with the power of their humanity, and left a profound impression in

---

6. Karol Wojtyla, *Nauczyciel i Pasterz, Listy pasterskie. Komunikaty. Zarzadzenia 1959–1978* (Rzym, 1987), pp. 89–91.

his soul." These were, for him, a demonstration of how much power in life is drawn from faith, and of how this power manifests itself above all in weakness.

The words he addressed to the sick overflowed with faith. In suffering lived together with Christ and for Christ, he saw a great redemptive value capable of enriching the entire community of the Church. "My dear brothers and sisters, I believe firmly in this truth," he told the sick.

> I make extensive use of this truth in my life and pastoral work as a bishop. If someone were to ask me what the foundation is for my pastoral ministry in the Archdiocese of Kraków, I would say that to a great extent it is based upon the truth that suffering, the trials through which many of our brothers and sisters pass, is the property of the entire Church— it is a good. This is what the Lord Jesus taught us; although suffering is an evil, for Christ and in Christ it is a good.... In fact, he accepted the passion and left us with the signs of this passion—not only the bloody external signs, but the interior ones as well: at Gethsemane, in his hour of agony on the cross, he left with us the marks of spiritual abandonment.... So, then, remember that you are like him, that we all want to become like him, watching you and drawing from you.[7]

---

7. Karol Wojtyla, *Kazania 1962–1978* (Kraków, 1979), p. 422.

He was always concerned, especially on the occasion of the World Days of the Sick or the spiritual retreats for the sick, that human suffering should be surrounded by human compassion, solidarity, and goodness. "We look upon you with love," Archbishop Karol Wojtyla said to the sick during his pastoral visit to one of the parishes. "We want to witness this love to you in our Christian community. At the same time, it is the duty of a parish to remember its sick and suffering members. This is the priests' duty, the sisters' duty, and they should dedicate themselves to carrying it out. But it is also the duty of the lay parishioners. One might say that this is the essence of the apostolate of the laity. The most ordinary, the simplest apostolate of the laity is precisely that of concern for the sick, for the suffering, for the abandoned and the needy."[8]

His life was always accompanied by thoughts on suffering, the cross, the fleeting nature of life, and death. Even his poetic works reflect this—but these thoughts did not become for him the cause of sadness, pessimism, or frustration. On the contrary, they drew him into a more intense interior life, to apostolic activity, and to a closer union with God, without which one cannot understand the full depths of the drama of human existence.

---

8. Czeslaw Drazek, SJ, *Caly dla Boga i ludzi; Habemus Papam* (Kraków, 1979), pp. 167–68.

The Pope of the Sick and the Suffering

Concern for the suffering, and especially for the sick, was one of the constant elements of John Paul II's pastoral activity from the beginning of his pontificate. He established a special bond with them immediately after his election to the Apostolic See. In his first *Urbi et Orbi* [to the city and to the world] message, which he delivered in the Sistine Chapel on October 17, 1978, he addressed himself to the sick with a very personal request: "The unworthy successor of Peter, who proposes to scrutinize the unfathomable riches of Christ, is in great need of your help, your prayers, and your sacrifices, and this I most humbly beg of you."[9] These words were not just niceties, but were full of love and trust. They expressed the new pope's profound conviction about the value, in the eyes of God, of suffering lived with Christ.

John Paul II returned to this theme during the afternoon of that same day, when he left the Vatican for Gemelli General Hospital to visit Bishop Andrzej Deskur, who was seriously ill, and to meet the other patients. It was an extremely moving visit. After a moment of prayer at his friend's sickbed, the Holy Father delivered an unrehearsed speech in the room where the patients, doctors, and nurses were gathered, revisiting the words he had spoken that morn-

---

9. *Insegnamenti di Giovanni Paolo II*, vol. I (1978) [op. cit.], p. 19.

ing to the cardinals on the meaning of human suffering in the light of faith. He then reminded the patients that, in spite of their weakened physical condition, they were "very powerful: powerful just like Jesus Christ crucified is powerful. This is how you resemble him. Strive to use this power for the good of the Church, your neighbors, your families, your country, and all of humanity. Use it also for the good of the ministry of the pope, who, in other ways, is also very weak."[10]

Both during his general audiences and in his visits to the Roman parishes, John Paul II always looked attentively at those in wheelchairs, the disabled, the elderly, the sick. He came up to them, talked with them, clasped their hands, blessed them, and asked for their spiritual support for his Petrine ministry. He wasn't indifferent toward any suffering person—he had a kind word and a compassionate gesture for everyone. He emphasized many times that Christ is present in those who suffer, and he always carried the meaning of this truth deep within himself, as he also carried the conviction that the salvation of the world and the conversion of man pass through the cross and human suffering.

The sick had a firm place in his interior life and were always present in his thoughts. "You already know," he said to the sick in Pompeii on October 21,

---

10. *L'Osservatore Romano*, October 19, 1978.

1979, "that the pope, in imitation of Jesus, whose Vicar he is on earth, has a special love for the sick and the suffering: consider this particular attention as one of the highest duties of his pastoral ministry."[11]

In planning for his first apostolic voyage, to Mexico, he wanted the numerous meetings with the faithful to include one with the sick. This took place in the Dominican church of Oaxaca, and it left a deep impression on the pope's memory and in his heart. After his trip, he said:

> I am grateful to those who organized this meeting, to the priests, the doctors, the hospital workers. Thanks to them, I was able to draw near to many sick persons, my brothers and sisters, in the land of Mexico. I was able to place my hand upon their heads, speak words of compassion and comfort to them, and ask for their prayers.
>
> I find great value in the prayer of the sick, in the intercession with God of those who suffer. They are so close to Christ! And I bring myself close to them, aware that Christ is present in them.
>
> The suffering of one's neighbor, the suffering of another person like me in every way, always raises a bit of discomfort in those who are not suffering, almost a sense of embarrassment. A question arises instinctively: why him and not me? It is not right to avoid this question, which is the elementary expression of human solidarity. I think it is this solidarity

---

11. *Insegnamenti di Giovanni Paolo II*, vol. II, book 2 (1979) (Vatican City: Libreria Editrice Vaticana, 1980), p. 820.

that gave rise to the practice of medicine and to all of the health services from their historical evolution until our own day.

So we must stop and pause before suffering, before the person who suffers, to rediscover this essential link between my sense of personhood and his own. We must pause before the person who suffers, to bear witness to the dignity of suffering— I should say to the majesty of suffering—to him and together with him as far as possible. We must bow our heads before our weak and defenseless brothers and sisters, who are deprived of what has been granted to us and what we enjoy every day.[12]

After his first voyage to Mexico, the plan for every one of his voyages, until his 104th to Lourdes, included a prominent place for the sick; their participation was the most important of all, as the pope affirmed. They were his most important helpers and collaborators in his service to the Church and the human family in the work of proclaiming the Gospel "to the ends of the earth" (Acts 1:8).

He entrusted every one of his apostolic voyages to the prayers and sacrifices of suffering persons. The photos of the pope meeting the sick often became the symbolic representation of the entire voyage. This is what happened during his trip to Brazil, where the Holy Father went to meet a few hundred

---

12. Angelus, February 11, 1979.

lepers at Marituba; in India, where his first steps in Calcutta were directed toward the hospice for the dying founded by Mother Teresa; in the United States, where in San Francisco, during the meeting with those sick with AIDS, he took into his arms a five-year-old boy who had been infected by a blood transfusion; in Mozambique, where he visited the wretched neighborhood on the outskirts of Maputo; in France, where in the Basilica of St. Martin of Tours he met a large group of men "wounded by life." With a clasp of hands and a warm word he greeted persons sick with AIDS, alcoholics, drug addicts, the homeless, the mentally handicapped, people marginalized by society. He recalled in his homily that every person is created in the image and likeness of God, and that nothing can erase this likeness. At the same time, he emphasized that the value of a society is determined by the way in which it treats its weakest and most suffering members.

"Do not forget the sick and the elderly," he said in Great Britain during the liturgy of the Anointing of the Sick in the cathedral of Southwark on May 28, 1982. "Do not abandon the handicapped and the seriously ill. Do not relegate them to the margins of society. If you do this, you ignore the fact that they embody an important truth. The sick, the elderly, the handicapped, and the infirm teach us that weakness is a creative part of human life and that suffering can be accepted without the loss of dignity.... The wisdom of Christ and the power of Christ are visible in the weakness of those who participate in his sufferings."[13]

Through his meetings with the sick, John Paul II united himself with every suffering person in the world: with all those who are weak, defenseless, and hungry; with those who are deprived of what properly belongs to them. He wanted to communicate his own love to them and express the gratitude of the Church, which sees in them the chosen portion of the People of God on its journey along the paths of history. For him, the model was Christ, who in announcing the commandment of love of neighbor put particular emphasis on the sick and identified himself with the "least brethren," making one's treatment of them the condition for attaining salvation (cf. Mt 25:34–40).

The pope's addresses to the sick inspired love, brought comfort, transmitted words of hope, and showed in the light of faith the Christian dimension of suffering, which is not blind destiny but has its place in the mystery of the divine plan of salvation. The truths he communicated were simple, evangelical, reaching the hearts of his listeners.

---

13. *Insegnamenti di Giovanni Paolo II*, vol. V, book 2 (1982) (Vatican City: Libreria Editrice Vaticana, 1982), p. 1911.

Speaking to the infirm, the pope also addressed those who care for them—doctors, nurses, pastors of souls, hospital chaplains, religious, young people—exhorting all to the generous service of their neighbor, according to the example of the Good Samaritan (cf. Lk 10:30–37), who was deeply moved when he saw a wounded man on the ground, drawing near to him and caring for him.

The many encounters between John Paul II and the sick, and his personal experience of suffering, found expression in the apostolic letter *Salvifici Doloris*, published on the feast of Our Lady of Lourdes on February 11, 1984. This extensive document—one of the most precious of the pope's teachings, prompted "by the deepest need of the heart, and also by the deep imperative of faith"—introduces us to what is perhaps the most difficult problem of human destiny among the great mysteries that recur in human reflection about the world, God, and life.

In this apostolic letter, the Holy Father expresses the Christian meaning of suffering which, lived together with the crucified and risen Christ, takes on enormous spiritual value, becomes a spiritual good for the Church and the world, and opens before man the treasures of grace and redemption. Through the sacrifices of the faithful, the Mystical Body grows, the whole Church is strengthened, and the witness of truth and love goes out to the whole world. The person in the wheelchair is just as necessary for the world as the engineers who build bridges, houses, or spacecrafts.

The suffering person *"is serving,* like Christ, *the salvation of his brothers and sisters.* Therefore he is carrying out an irreplaceable service. In the Body of Christ, which is ceaselessly born of the cross of the Redeemer, it is precisely suffering permeated by the spirit of Christ's sacrifice that is *the irreplaceable mediator and author of the good things* which are indispensable for the world's salvation. It is suffering, more than anything else, which clears the way for the grace which transforms human souls. Suffering, more than anything else, makes present in the history of humanity the powers of the Redemption."[14]

In this context, the Holy Father speaks of suffering as a vocation. Christ, who suffered torment and drained to the last drop the bitter cup given to him by the Father, addresses every suffering person with the words "Follow me!" As a person gradually responds to the Savior's call, entrusting oneself deliberately into the hands of Jesus; as that person gradually unites one's own cross with that of Jesus, he or she discovers the deepest meaning of suffering and transforms it into a creative force. Together, they save the world. In this way, suffering makes possible a spe-

---

14. *Salvifici Doloris,* no. 27.

cial kind of contact with God and becomes prayer. Human spirituality does not remain subjected to the limitations of time, space, and human power, but enters into the salvific work of Christ, being infinitely multiplied in him and extending everywhere.

In light of John Paul II's letter, suffering does not appear as a purely negative reality, but is seen as "a visitation from God," granted in order "to give birth to works of love toward neighbor, in order to transform the whole of human civilization into a 'civilization of love.'"[15] The world of human suffering opens the way to the world of human love.

The letter was received very gladly by the family of the sick all over the world, because everyone knew that he had written it as the successor of Peter, who had followed the path of suffering himself, abandoned to the care and help of others.

In consideration of those tried by physical suffering, John Paul II began important apostolic activities in the Church in order to sensitize consciences about the dramatic plight of the suffering, and in order to stir up love for them among families and in society. On the first anniversary of the publication of the letter *Salvifici Doloris,* the Holy Father released the *motu proprio Dolentium Hominum* and created the Commission for Pastoral Assistance to Health Workers. The

---

15. *Salvifici Doloris,* no. 30.

task of this new institution of the Holy See is the perfecting and expansion of material and spiritual resources for the sick, and the coordination of the work of all Church-run health institutions.

Similar aims inspired the World Day of the Sick, instituted by John Paul II on May 13, 1992, and celebrated by the Church on the feast of Our Lady of Lourdes. Beginning in 1980, the pope met on this day with sick people in the Vatican basilica, and from this practice, which was so greatly appreciated by the sick and their caregivers, was born the idea of organizing similar meetings in the universal Church. The observance of this day is, in part, meant to sensitize the entire People of God to the necessity of assuring the best care possible for the sick and of helping them to discover the human and Christian value of suffering. It is also meant to support the pastoral care of the sick in the dioceses, parishes, communities of consecrated life, etc.

The World Day of the Sick is an appeal addressed to persons, groups, and national and international institutions, to make a priority of the problems of health care in a new world order, based upon solidarity and the collaboration of all peoples and nations. The message for the World Day of the Sick that the pope published every year called for public attention to the great reality of human suffering, and it invited all to work together to respond effectively to the yearnings of their brothers and sisters immersed in sadness and pain. It is not right "to pass them by," the pope taught, but one must pause and, in the spirit of sacrifice, take upon oneself a part of their burden. Human life is a gift, and it does not cease to be precious even when it is marked by physical weakness and limitations.

The World Day of the Sick is an occasion for a new evangelization of suffering, for spiritual renewal and authentic Christian witness. It is an occasion for bishops, priests, and religious who give pastoral care, and also for the lay faithful: doctors, nurses, the volunteers who work in hospitals and rest homes. We must love others and place at their service the life we have received as a free gift from God.

John Paul II's teaching and actions in regard to those who suffer is a coherent realization of the plan he himself proposed in the encyclical *Redemptor Hominis,* which asked for respect on behalf of every human person, especially for the weak and defenseless who are identified with Christ. "Man is the primary route that the Church must travel in fulfilling her mission: *he is the primary and fundamental way for the Church,* the way traced out by Christ himself, the way that leads invariably through the mystery of the Incarnation and the Redemption."[16]

---

16. *Redemptor Hominis,* no. 14.

The Holy Father did not spare any of his strength, heart, prayer, or sacrifice in the full realization of this plan.

At the Shrine of Pain and Hope

The bond between John Paul II and those who carry the weight of the cross was reinforced even more on the day his pontificate was marked more than any other by blood and lengthy suffering. On May 13, 1981, during the general audience in St. Peter's Square, Mehmet Ali Agca shot the Holy Father, wounding him severely in the abdomen and in his left elbow and index finger. If there had not been immediate action, which permitted doctors to begin surgery at the Gemelli Hospital within half an hour of the attack, there could have been dangerous complications, including extensive internal hemorrhaging leading to death. The operation, which lasted for five hours and was directed by surgical professor Francesco Crucitti, involved stitching up the pope's ruptured colon, removing a damaged portion of his intestine, and applying a temporary colostomy.

The Holy Father suffered greatly. He prayed constantly. He remained in intensive care for four days, then was transferred to a room prepared for him on the tenth floor. For many days he experienced what he had been talking about, with sensitivity and tenderness, in his many speeches to the sick, as well as what he had observed during his many meetings with them: powerlessness, weakness, pain, sadness, isolation, and dependence upon others.

He drew strength from his personal and liturgical prayer. It was a great comfort to him that prayers for his health were being offered incessantly all over the world, as the first Christians had done in Jerusalem, offering this help to Peter when his life was in danger (cf. Acts 12:5).

In his first words to the faithful after the attack, John Paul spoke from his heart in a faint voice: "With great emotion I thank you for your prayers, and I bless you all. I am particularly close to the two persons who were wounded together with me. I pray for the brother who wounded me, whom I have sincerely forgiven. United with Christ, priest and victim, I offer my sufferings for the Church and the world. To you, Mary, I repeat: *Totus tuus ego sum* [I am entirely yours]."[17]

The attack upon the Holy Father and his sufferings shook the consciousness of people around the world. Believers and non-believers united during those dramatic days in fear, anguish, and hope. The Vatican received countless letters and telegrams from all over the world, with best wishes for the pope from

---

17. *Regina Coeli*, May 17, 1981.

heads of state, international organizations, representatives of all kinds of religious confessions, and ordinary people. Visitors and pilgrims gathered daily outside Gemelli Hospital and in its lobby, a visible sign of closeness and solidarity with the successor of Peter. On June 3, John Paul II returned to the Vatican.

His health declined after a few days. He suffered from a fever and severe pain. His consulting physicians decided that he again needed to be hospitalized. On June 20, the pope had to return to the Gemelli Hospital. Microbiological examinations revealed an inflammation caused by the presence of cytomegalovirus.

When the Holy Father felt better, Doctor Crucitti removed the colostomy. Postoperative recovery was favorable.

Before leaving the hospital on August 14, John Paul II expressed in a speech to the sick his gratitude to God for the gift of having saved his life, and "for having been granted, over the course of those three months, to belong...to the community of the sick suffering in that hospital, who constitute, in a certain sense, a special segment of the Church, of the Mystical Body of Christ."[18] In his brief and unrehearsed greeting when he returned to the Vatican, he

---

18. *Insegnamenti di Giovanni Paolo II*, vol. II, book 2 (1981) (Vatican City: Libreria Editrice Vaticana, 1982), p. 81.

said what no one dared to think: that everything could have turned out differently, and that the Vatican basilica "might have had one more tomb added. But the Lord worked differently, and our Lady—we all remember it was May 13—played a part in that 'difference.'"[19]

When, after five months of illness and recovery, the pope returned to St. Peter's Square, he fervently thanked all those who had contributed to saving his life and everyone throughout the world who had immersed him in a powerful wave of prayer. Over the course of a few general audiences, he also revealed to us the deep, mysterious spiritual experiences he had undergone during his recovery in the hospital, as a sick man among the sick.

> Could I forget that the event in St. Peter's Square took place on the day and at the time when, for over sixty years, we have commemorated the first apparition of the Mother of Christ to the humble rural children in Fatima, Portugal? In everything that happened to me that day, I felt her extraordinary protection and concern, which showed itself to be more powerful than the assassin's bullet.[20]
>
> During the past few months, God permitted me to experience suffering; he permitted me to experience the danger of losing my life. He also permit-

---

19. Ibid., p. 84.
20. General Audience, October 7, 1981.

ted me to understand clearly and fully that this is his special grace for me as a man, and at the same time—in consideration of the service that I carry out as bishop of Rome and successor of St. Peter—a grace for the Church.[21]

My personal experience of violence has made me feel more intensely my closeness to those who, in any place on the earth and in whatever way, suffer persecutions for the sake of Christ. It also made me feel closer to those who suffer oppression for the holy cause of human dignity, for justice and peace in the world. And finally, it has brought me near to those who have sealed their faithfulness with death.[22]

The memory of that event always remained in John Paul II's heart. He always revisited it in prayer, especially on the anniversary of the attack, celebrating a Holy Mass of thanksgiving in the afternoon in his private chapel. In his will, he expressed his deepest conviction, which he had never abandoned:

On May 13, 1981, the day of the attack on the pope during the general audience in St. Peter's Square, divine Providence saved me from death in a miraculous way. He who is the only Lord of life and death, he himself prolonged my life, and in a certain way he gave it back to me again. From that moment on, my life belonged to him all the more.[23]

---

21. General Audience, October 14, 1981.
22. General Audience, October 28, 1981.
23. *L'Osservatore Romano*, April 8, 2005, p. 3.

Although he had fallen victim to an attack that scarred him for the rest of his life, John Paul II did not change the style of his pastoral ministry after his injury. Driven by the love of Christ, he did not spare himself in proclaiming the Gospel to all the nations, in strengthening his brethren in the faith, in bringing consolation to people and going to meet those who suffer.

But the attack and the surgery following it did in fact weaken the pope's health and physical strength. He began to be tormented by illnesses, which he did not conceal. On July 12, 1992, during the Sunday Angelus address, he "confided" that he had needed to visit the Gemelli for medical tests the evening before. The news quickly spread all over the world, raising general concern. On the day of the attack, suffering had taken a prominent place in the Holy Father's life. This time it showed its true face and was even more striking. John Paul II, who was for many the symbol of physical vigor and untiring activity, suddenly presented himself to the world as a man tried by illness, as a big brother whose health, in spite of his natural robustness, was now weakened by fatigue and by the trials of the years gone by.

Diagnostic exams revealed a sizable tumor in his large intestine, and surgery was necessary. When someone in his inner circle spoke of the suffering involved in the operation scheduled for July 15, the

Holy Father replied: "The Church needs suffering." On another occasion he added: "What are my sufferings compared with the sufferings of Jesus?" During his recovery in the hospital, the Holy Father celebrated the Eucharist every day in his bed, and later, when he felt better, seated on a couch.

He also thanked the faithful for their prayers, "the most welcome gift and the most effective way to live life's moments of difficulty and suffering with faith and serenity."[24]

The sentiments that ran through the whole world during those days can be found in the prayer composed by Mother Teresa of Calcutta for this man of peace, universal harmony, and boundless love for God and others:

> O Lord, once again you have wanted
> our Pope John Paul II
> beside you on the cross,
> to remind the world
> that only in the cross is there resurrection
>   and life.
> Through the cross you remind us
> that you have redeemed the world.
> The disciple of Christ knows
> that the work of Redemption continues in time
> and in the life of every man and woman

---

24. Angelus, July 19, 1992.

only through the embrace of the cross.
With the ailing pope in the hospital, you,
   O Lord,
show us how he, too, crucified in the flesh,
unites himself with all those in the world
who bear the marks of the passion
   of Jesus Christ.
Under the weight of the cross,
the pope, following the example of Jesus,
teaches us to "love" the cross.
The Christian's cross is always a holy cross:
teach us, O Lord, to stand beneath
the wood of the cross.
After the cross, O Lord,
comes the radiant dawn
of the resurrection.
Our Holy Father
saw this dawn of the resurrection
in May of 1981, after he lived through
the dark night of that tragic event.
As then, so also today
the pope will return to serve the Church,
after expressing his love for it once again
at the foot of the cross.
O Lord, give John Paul II
new strength to serve the Church
and all the people of the world.
Give him the joy

of being able to clasp the hands
of children, orphans, widows,
and the least of the world.
The Holy Father is for us presence,
he is grace, he is hope, he is certitude.
O Lord, do not let our certainty be crushed,
above all in the moments of pain and trial.
Thank you, O Lord, for how much
  you love us.[25]

John Paul II left the hospital on July 28, and, after a period of convalescence, resumed his pastoral ministry, but the Lord continued to ask for this offering which, as the pope wrote in *Salvifici Doloris,* is "a source of strength for the Church and humanity,"[26] and this includes the means of physical suffering. After a short time he returned twice more to Gemelli Hospital. The first time (April 29–May 27, 1994) was after he broke his right femur, which made it necessary to implant a prosthetic hip joint. The second time (from October 6–15, 1996) was for an appendectomy.

His recovery in the hospital, in this "Vatican III"—as he put it—and "this other 'shrine'...where tears of pain and hope are poured out every day,"[27]

---

25. *L'Osservatore Romano,* August 24, 1992, p. 1.
26. *Salvifici Doloris,* no. 31.
27. Angelus, May 1, 1994.

permitted us to understand better the value of the Petrine ministry in the context of the Church's preparation for the Great Jubilee of the Year 2000, and also for the celebration of the Year of the Family.

Through the mysterious design of divine Providence, this ministry also expressed itself through the gift of physical suffering. After his return from the hospital in 1994 he said,

> I understand that I must bring the Church of Christ into this third millennium with prayer and various initiatives, but I have seen that this is not enough: it must be brought in with suffering, with the attack of thirteen years ago and with this new sacrifice. Why now, why this year, why during this Year of the Family? Precisely because the family is threatened, the family is under attack. The pope must be attacked, the pope must suffer, so that all families and the world may see that there is what I call a "higher Gospel": the Gospel of suffering, with which we must prepare the future, the third millennium of families, of each family and all families together.[28]

The last years, months, and weeks of John Paul II's ministry of love were marked by pain, by the inability to walk, by difficulty in speaking, by the cross that he carried serenely and with extraordinary

---

28. Angelus, May 29, 1994.

strength, patience, and trust in Christ and his Mother. Through suffering and the cross, the pope participated in the Church's struggle against everything opposed to its mission in the modern world: atheism, religious indifference, secularism, consumerism, the civilization of death. The Holy Father's infirmity revealed more deeply who he was for all people of the world, whom he accompanied with prayer amid his physical weakness, offering expressions of particular closeness and participation.

The pope's suffering united the Church around the successor of Peter. This was seen in an extraordinary way during his last stays at the Gemelli Hospital (from February 1–10 and from February 24–March 13, 2005). Complications arising from the flu required his hospitalization for over a week, and after this, when his breathing difficulties increased, the Holy Father returned to the hospital and underwent a tracheotomy. As soon as he revived from the anesthesia, with great emotion he wrote "*Totus tuus*" on a piece of paper, abandoning his whole life once again to Mary.

As during his previous stays at the hospital, so also this time he celebrated the Eucharist every day, recited the breviary, the Angelus, the Rosary, the Stations of the Cross. He dedicated time to spiritual reading and prayed before the Most Holy Sacrament in his private chapel.

"Even here in the hospital," he stated, "in the midst of other sick people...I continue to serve the Church and all of humanity."[29]

"It is by watching Christ and following him with patient trust that we are able to understand how every form of human pain contains within itself a divine promise of salvation and glory. I would like this message of comfort and hope to reach all, especially those experiencing moments of difficulty, those who suffer in body and spirit."[30]

People accepted these messages with great emotion, knowing that they were being communicated by someone who understood them well, who loved them, who offered his sufferings for them and was always with them. Someone remarked that, during his illness, the pope was writing "an encyclical without words," that he was proclaiming to all the love of Christ, who by dying on the cross accomplished the Father's plan and redeemed the world.

During his visit to Gemelli Hospital in Rome, Benedict XVI had profound words to say about the suffering and illness of his predecessor:

> Finding ourselves together here, my dear and illustrious friends, we cannot help but think of the

29. Angelus, February 6, 2005.
30. Angelus, February 27, 2005.

moments full of trepidation and emotion that we experienced during John Paul II's final stay at this hospital. During those days, the thoughts of Catholics all over the world—and not only of Catholics—were directed toward the Gemelli. From his hospital rooms, the pope imparted to all an incomparable lesson on the Christian meaning of life and suffering, witnessing in person to the truth of the Christian message.[31]

Toward the Father's House

John Paul II's profound union with God and his participation in the paschal mystery fully revealed themselves in the last days of his life. His body continued to weaken, until he was utterly deprived of strength and brought to obedience "to the point of death" (cf. Phil 2:8), but he remained strong in spirit and "loved until the end" (cf. Jn 13:1).

For the first time in twenty-six years, the pope was not able to preside over the rites of the Easter Triduum, although he ardently desired to do so. He sought to be present to the faithful by sending them brief meditations, which were read during the liturgies of Holy Week.

"I am spiritually with you at the Colosseum," he wrote in the Good Friday message intended for those participating in the Way of the Cross ceremony

---

31. *L'Osservatore Romano*, November 26, 2005, p. 5.

broadcast around the world, adding words that reveal the interior disposition with which he faced all his sufferings:

> The veneration of the cross brings us back to a commitment that we must not avoid. It is the mission that St. Paul expressed with the words, "In my flesh I am completing what is lacking in Christ's afflictions for the sake of his body, that is, the Church" (Col 1:24). I also offer up my own sufferings, that the plan of God may be accomplished and his word may spread among the peoples. And I am close to those who, at this moment, are being tried by suffering. I pray for each of them.
>
> On this day, the memorial of Christ's crucifixion, together with you I look upon and adore the cross and repeat the words of the liturgy: *O Crux, ave spes unica!* Hail, O Cross, our only hope; give us patience and courage, and obtain peace for the world![32]

The Holy Father was seated before the altar of his private chapel, following the celebration on a television set placed near him, and he prayed and meditated on each of the stations of the Lord's passion. At the fourteenth station, he took the crucifix in his hands and pressed his suffering-stricken face to it, as if to say—like Peter—"Lord, you know everything; you know that I love you" (Jn 21:17).

---

32. *L'Osservatore Romano,* March 27, 2005, p. 5.

The love of Christ that is stronger than death comforted his spirit, and he wanted to express this on Easter Sunday, when at midday he appeared at the window of his private library to impart the apostolic blessing *Urbi et Orbi* to the multitudes gathered in St. Peter's Square and to all those who had participated in the liturgy by television. Because of his deep emotion and his suffering, he was unable to speak, and only made the Sign of the Cross and responded with a wave to the greetings of the faithful. This gesture of powerlessness, of suffering and fatherly love, together with the touching silence of the successor of Peter, left an indelible impression in the hearts of people all over the world.

The Holy Father was also profoundly shaken by this event. After he moved away from the window, he said: "Maybe it would be better for me to die if I cannot carry out the mission entrusted to me," and immediately added: "Your will be done.... *Totus tuus.*" He had wished for nothing else in his life.

He wasn't afraid of dying. Christ had been his guide all his life, and John Paul knew he was going to meet him. During the celebrations of the Great Jubilee of the Year 2000, he wrote in his will: "I ask him to call me back when he himself chooses. 'In life and death, we belong to the Lord.... We are the Lord's' (cf. Rom 14:8)."[33] He had always been profoundly

---

33. *L'Osservatore Romano*, April 8, 2005, p. 3.

aware that at the end of his earthly pilgrimage man is not doomed to fall into darkness, into an existential void or an abyss of nothingness, but is called rather to meet the best of fathers, who welcomes his child lovingly into his arms, giving him the fullness of life in the Most Holy Trinity.

Knowing that his time to pass to eternity was coming, in agreement with his doctors the pope had decided not to go to the hospital but to remain in the Vatican, where the essential medical equipment and procedures had been prepared. He wanted to suffer and die at home, remaining near the tomb of the Apostle Peter.

The last day of his life—Saturday, April 2—he said goodbye to his closest collaborators in the Roman Curia. Prayers continued in his private chapel, and he joined along in spite of his high fever and extreme weakness. At a certain moment in the afternoon, he said, "Let me go to the house of the Father." Around 5:00 P.M., there was the recitation of the first Vespers of the Second Sunday of Easter, Divine Mercy Sunday. The readings spoke of the empty tomb and the resurrection of Christ, with the recurrence of the word "Alleluia." At the end was the recitation of the Magnificat and the *Salve Regina*. The Holy Father repeatedly embraced with his gaze those of his closest circle who were present, and the doctors who were watching over him nearby. From

St. Peter's Square, where thousands of the faithful had gathered, especially young people, there came shouts of "John Paul II" and "Long live the Pope!" He could hear these words. On the wall facing the Holy Father's bed was a painting of the suffering Christ bound with ropes, the *Ecce Homo*, which John Paul gazed upon intently all through his illness. The eyes of the dying pope also rested upon an image of Our Lady of Czestochowa. A little bedside table held a photograph of his parents.

At around 8:00 P.M. beside the pope's bed, Archbishop Stanislaw Dziwisz presided over Holy Mass for Divine Mercy Sunday. The concelebrants included Cardinal Marian Jaworski, Archbishop Stanislaw Rylko, Monsignor Mieczyslaw Mokrzycki, and Father Tadeusz Styczen. The other participants were Doctor Renato Buzzonetti, his collaborators, and the Sacred Heart Sisters of the pontifical household.

The words of the Gospel of St. John rang out with special emotional impact: "Jesus came, and standing in their midst said to them: 'Peace be with you!'," as did the words of the universal prayer: "Lord Jesus, come to make us hear the promise you made to us in the upper room: 'Peace be with you!' In this moment, we are in great need of your presence."

Before the offertory, Cardinal Marian Jaworski once again administered the Anointing of the Sick to the Holy Father, and during communion Archbishop

Dziwisz gave him the Most Precious Blood as viaticum, as strength for his journey to eternal life. After a little while, the Holy Father's strength began to leave him. A blessed and lighted candle was placed in his hand. At 9:37 P.M., John Paul II departed from this earth. Those who were present sang the *Te Deum*. With tears in their eyes, they gave thanks to God for the gift of the Holy Father and for his tremendous pontificate.

Conclusion

John Paul II passed "from life into life" on the day dedicated to Mary—the first Saturday of the month—and on the liturgical feast of Divine Mercy. This passage to eternity, which had seen the participation of the entire human family, was John Paul II's last catechesis. In it, he taught that moments of suffering and death must be lived in the light of faith, with Christian love and hope, in complete abandonment to the will of God, serving the Church and the salvation of humanity until the very end.

The Church and the world heard and remembered this silent catechesis, which was the summit of the teaching ministry of this servant of God. On December 22, 2005, on the occasion of the exchange of Christmas greetings, Benedict XVI addressed the Roman Curia at the Vatican, and it is with his magnificent testimony that we wish to conclude our reflection:

> No pope has left us such a quantity of texts as he has bequeathed to us; no previous pope was able to visit the whole world like him and speak directly to people from all the continents. In the end, however, his lot was a journey of suffering and silence. With his words and actions, the Holy Father gave us great things; equally important is the lesson he imparted to us from the chair of suffering and silence. In his last book, *Memory and Identity* (Weidenfeld and Nicolson, 2005), he has left us an interpretation of suffering that is not a theological or philosophical theory but a fruit that matured on his personal path of suffering which he walked, sustained by faith in the Crucified Lord. This interpretation, which he worked out in faith and which gave meaning to his suffering lived in communion with that of the Lord, spoke through his silent pain, transforming it into an important message. Both at the beginning and once again at the end of the book mentioned, the pope shows that he is deeply touched by the spectacle of the power of evil, which we dramatically experienced in the century that has just ended.
>
> He says in his text: "The evil...was not a small-scale evil.... It was an evil of gigantic proportions, an evil which availed itself of state structures in order to accomplish its wicked work, an evil built up into a system" (p. 189). Might evil be invincible? Is it the ultimate power of history? Because of the experi-

ence of evil, for Pope Wojtyla the question of redemption became the essential and central question of his life and thought as a Christian. Is there a limit against which the power of evil shatters? "Yes, there is," the pope replies in this book of his, as well as in his encyclical on Redemption. The power that imposes a limit on evil is Divine Mercy. Violence, the display of evil, is opposed in history—as "the totally other" of God, God's own power—by Divine Mercy. The Lamb is stronger than the dragon, we could say together with the Book of Revelation.

At the end of the book, in a retrospective review of the attack of May 13, 1981, and on the basis of the experience of his journey with God and with the world, John Paul II further deepened this answer. What limits the force of evil, the power, in brief, which overcomes it—this is how he says it—is God's suffering, the suffering of the Son of God on the cross: "The suffering of the Crucified God is not just one form of suffering alongside others.... In sacrificing himself for us all, Christ gave new meaning to suffering, opening up a new dimension, a new order: the order of love.... The passion of Christ on the cross gave a radically new meaning to suffering, transforming it from within.... It is this suffering which burns and consumes evil with the flame of love.... All human suffering, all pain, all infirmity contains within itself a promise of salvation...; evil is present in the world partly so as to awaken our love, our self-gift in generous and disinterested service to those visited by suffering.... Christ has redeemed the world: 'By his wounds we are healed' (Is 53:5)" (p. 189ff.). All this is not merely learned theology, but the expression of a faith lived and matured through suffering. Of course, we must do all we can to alleviate suffering and prevent the injustice that causes the suffering of the innocent. However, we must also do the utmost to ensure that people can discover the meaning of suffering and are thus able to accept their own suffering and to unite it with the suffering of Christ. In this way, it is merged with redemptive love and consequently becomes a force against the evil in the world. The response across the world to the pope's death was an overwhelming demonstration of gratitude for the fact that in his ministry he offered himself totally to God for the world; a thanksgiving for the fact that in a world full of hatred and violence he taught anew love and suffering in the service of others; he showed us, so to speak, in the flesh, the Redeemer, redemption, and gave us the certainty that indeed evil does not have the last word in the world.[34]

---

34. *L'Osservatore Romano*, December 23, 2005, p. 4 [translation from www.vatican.va].

THE DAYS OF
SUFFERING AND HOPE

by Renato Buzzonetti

Personal physician of
His Holiness John Paul II

A T 5:19 P.M. ON WEDNESDAY, May 13, 1981, two gunshots rang out in St. Peter's Square, striking John Paul II. The pope was riding in a white jeep through the right side of the square, where a large crowd of the faithful was gathered for the regular Wednesday general audience. There were six doctors stationed nearby with their assistants and two ambulances. Doctor Alessandro Sabato, an emergency physician among the Holy Father's medical team, began to follow the ambulances, but they sped away from the square and through the Arco delle Campane. They passed along the Via delle Fondamenta, which extends around the apse of the Vatican basilica, went down past the "Grottone," and passed through the

Belvedere courtyard, finally reaching the Vatican's health facilities.

It was here that I was alerted by the doctor stationed in front of the bronze gate. As the personal physician of His Holiness, I was ready to attend to the Holy Father, together with other health professionals. By a series of lucky or providential coincidences, I had delayed going down to the square.

The pope was brought into the clinic entryway, where I immediately met him. He was conscious, could respond to simple commands and move his legs, and all of his arteries had pressure. A small red stain was visible on the cincture around his white robes. The Holy Father was then placed upon a gurney from one of the two ambulances. The ambulance left at 5:29 and went through the Sant'Anna gate, heading toward Gemelli Hospital on my orders, which had been confirmed by his secretary. During the trip, the ambulance siren failed, and the driver had to resort to desperately honking the horn.

The pope's vestments were opened up, revealing his blood-soaked pants, a fracture of the tip of the second finger on his left hand, and a gash along his right elbow. His blood pressure had dropped during his transport, without reaching critical levels.

In the ambulance, the Holy Father let out faint cries and ceaselessly invoked, in Polish, "Jesus, Mary my mother."

At 5:36, the ambulance arrived at Agostino Gemelli University Hospital. In spite of my emphatic requests to bring him to an operating room right away, the patient was taken to the tenth floor, to the room that had been set aside since 1979 for all of the Holy Father's emergency hospitalizations. Here immediate procedures were carried out, and he was inspected by the surgeon on duty, Doctor Alfredo Wiel-Marin. The pope's skin was sweaty and cold, his blood pressure had further fallen, and his mind was foggy. The pope was immediately brought to the operating room, and two doors were broken down to shorten the path.

At 5:50, the Holy Father was on the operating table of room D in operating block fifty on the ninth floor, and general anesthesia was administered.

On my advice, Archbishop Stanislaw Dziwisz imparted to the Holy Father, who may have been unconscious, the Anointing of the Sick and absolution.

It is interesting to note that the operating room was already prepared for a scheduled elective procedure, and most of the necessary staff were already in place. The anesthesia, which had been begun by Doctor Francesco Beccia, was conducted and directed by Doctor Corrado Manni, Director of the Institute of Anesthesia and Emergency Care at the Catholic University of the Sacred Heart, who had arrived in the meantime. The preliminary phases of the operation were performed by Doctor Giovanni Salgarello, the assisting physician of the surgical clinic. The operation as a whole was personally carried out and brought to a happy conclusion by Doctor Francesco Crucitti, the principal diagnostician at Gemelli Hospital and the substitute for Doctor Gian Carlo Castiglioni, Director of the Institute of Surgical Studies, who was away from Rome at the time.

Doctor Crucitti had been working at a clinic in Rome; when he heard what had happened from a religious sister, he raced by car to the Gemelli, asking a motorcycle policeman to clear the way for him. In effect, the personnel of the surgical clinic were on duty that day, and Doctor Crucitti rightly felt responsible for directing the operation. After 7:00 P.M., Doctor Castiglioni arrived from Milan, and he carried out part of the operation. Cardiovasculary assistance was provided by Doctor Ugo Manzoli, Director of the Institute of Cardiology at Catholic University. The operation required a transfusion of 3,150 ml of blood, the first portion of which came from the pediatric hospital Bambino Gesù where a stockpile had been prudently reserved for the pope since 1979.

This operation was made necessary by the multiple internal wounds caused by the bullet, which had passed along the abdominal and spinal area. Damage was shown to the small intestine, the colon, and the peritoneum, and there was a massive abdominal hemorrhage. There was also a contusion on the right forearm and two fractures of the second finger of the right hand.

A temporary colostomy was put in place. Providentially, the murderous bullet had not penetrated the abdominal aorta or the spinal column.

The operation was concluded at 11:25 P.M. and was recorded under number 750 of the operating log. At 12.05 A.M. on Thursday, May 14, the Holy Father was brought to the Bianca Rosa Fanfani Intensive Care Unit, where order and silence reigned. Throughout the night, the Holy Father was watched over by the ward staff, but also by his secretary, by Sister Tobiana Sobotka, the superior of the religious order at the hospital, and by myself. In the early hours of the morning, the pope fully regained consciousness, and his first words were "pain...thirst," and then, "like Bachelet." Vittorio Bachelet, the vice-president of the Superior Council of the Magistrature and former president of Italian Catholic Action, had been killed by the Red Brigade. The pope would mention this comparison a number of times over the following days.

At dawn, the pope said to his secretary, "Yesterday we did not recite Compline," and then listened as the prayers of the night before were read.

All of the doctors, nurses, and staff of the hospital streamed to the Holy Father's bedside. The young nurses in particular spent whole hours of the night next to the injured pope's bed.

On May 14, the group of doctors responsible for the pope's care was composed: it included Doctors Castiglioni, Crucitti, Manni, Manzoli, Breda (the clinical doctor), and Buzzonetti.

During the afternoon of Thursday, May 14, the Holy Father concelebrated Holy Mass from his bed.

The following Sunday, May 17, he donned a stole and celebrated Mass. The entrance to his room was opened, and staff members of the hospital were present. After the Mass, the pope recorded his greeting for the *Regina Coeli,* which was later broadcast on Vatican Radio.

At 12:10 A.M. on Monday, May 18, the day of his sixty-first birthday, I offered my best wishes to the Holy Father and later gave him a red rose on behalf of my wife and children. That same day, the injured pope was transferred to the tenth floor of the hospital, to a fully equipped recovery room. This had been arranged since 1979, following my discussions with the rector of the university, Doctor Giuseppe Lazzati. As he left, the Holy Father said goodbye to all the staff of the intensive care unit, saying in part, "The doctor and the priest both touch the eschatological dimension of man and help man to cross the mysterious frontier of death."

On Tuesday, May 19, during the afternoon, a medical consultation took place that had been proposed by the secretary of state and the Polish cardinals. There was participation from clinicians of international stature, such as Doctor Loygue of the medical faculty of St. Anthony of Paris, Doctor Bunte of the University of Münster, Doctor Welch of Boston, Doctor Cahill of New York, Doctor Turowski of the Copernicus Academy of Medicine in Kraków, and Doctor Vilardell of the Hospital of St. Paul and the Holy Cross in Barcelona. The consultants were received by the Holy Father and were deeply moved by the kind greeting that the injured man offered each person present in his own language.

The consultation ended with an explicit and public expression of satisfaction with the results of the operation and with the therapeutic means taken.

On May 23, the consulting group reached its confidential prognosis.

On the evening of June 3, at 7:10 P.M., a pallid and shaken Holy Father returned to the Vatican after twenty-one days of convalescence. But he quickly displayed new signs of a fever, which had already shown up during his last days of recovery at the Gemelli. A diagnostic procedure involved, among other things, an ultrasound of the pope's abdomen, which was conducted in the library of the pope's apartment. The pope had a high fever; his inner circle of advisers was full of concern and vague fears, and the doctors were posing some alarming questions to each other. But the exam had to be interrupted because of electronic interference from Vatican Radio antennae. Only the personal intervention of the deputy secretary of state was able to convince the directors of the radio station, who were afraid of an act of sabotage by the Red Brigade, to briefly suspend their broadcasts with the announcement of a nonexistent technical difficulty. The exam was completed, but the results were unclear.

In order to determine the exact nature of the fever, the pope was brought back to the Gemelli on June 20. Here, following laboratory analyses, the diagnosis was made of a cytomegalovirus infection.

Under these circumstances, other specialists were called in as members of the medical group caring for the pope. These were Doctor Luisi Ortona, Director of the Institute of Infectious Diseases at Catholic University; Doctor Giancarlo Fegiz, a surgeon; and Doctor Giuseppe Giunchi, a clinician at La Sapienza University in Rome.

The attack, the difficult surgical procedure, the complications due to infection, and the long recovery period in the hospital made an indelible mark in the mind and heart of the pope. After he passed through these critical phases, he burned with the desire to return to his post of duty at least in time, he said, for the second half of August, when the members of the curia finish their vacation.

With this hope, the pope attended the meeting of his medical team on the evening of July 21 at the Gemelli. He was in splendid form, and while he acknowledged that he was not competent in medical questions, he asserted the right of the sick person— his right—to be an active participant in the management of his illness, and not just a passive recipient. He added that he would accept his part of the risk, and that he would not leave the hospital before the second and conclusive operation. Finally, he asked that this last stage not be drawn out, to avoid continuing delays of his many tasks, including resumption of the *ad limina* visits.

On August 5, Doctor Crucitti carried out the operation to remove the colostomy.

After recuperating at the hospital, at 10:10 P.M. on August 14, the vigil of the solemnity of the Assumption, John Paul II returned to the Vatican after his dramatic experience of dangerous complications and reassuring interludes, of barely concealed tensions and silent, diligent dedication. A long period of convalescence followed at his summer residence in Castel Gandolfo.

On Wednesday morning, October 7, the pope returned to St. Peter's Square in his white jeep for the general audience.

—◆—

Let's step back for a moment. On the evening of December 29, 1978, while I was at work at my station in the hospital of San Camillo, which was at the time the largest medical facility in Rome, I was surprised to be summoned to the pope's private apartment on the third floor of the apostolic palace. For about thirteen years I had belonged to the medical staff of Vatican City, which is composed of doctors rendering part-time service. But I had no idea that, without any forewarning, I would be brought into the presence of John Paul II.

The pope, with a few quick words in his still-halting Italian, asked me to become his personal physician and quickly gave me a concise summary of his medical history. And so began for me a professional and spiritual adventure that lasted almost twenty-seven years.

And I had no way of guessing on that day—now long ago—that, almost two years later, I would be directly involved in the tragic event of the attack that brought the pope to the brink of death and inflicted a hideous wound upon the heart of the Church and the awareness of the entire world.

———◆———

At the beginning of January 1979, John Paul had patiently subjected himself to an exhaustive medical checkup in preparation for his first international voyage as pope, which brought him to Mexico. In time, this would be followed by clinical examinations at the rate of approximately one every six months.

The pope's resumption of activities quickly became extremely energetic. His good physical constitution and his impressive apostolic zeal permitted the Holy Father to carry out extensive intellectual work, a bustling ministry as head and shepherd of the Vatican, Rome, and of the world, and an interior life characterized by unceasing prayer.

The years immediately following his injury were not marked by any significant medical problems. The pope's health was good, and he was able to face his fast-paced life and tremendous responsibilities with a tenacious and sometimes stubborn sense of commitment, even when bodily fatigue and mental stress were weighing upon him. As early as 1979, he confessed that the Wednesday general audiences were very tiring.

But with the passing of years, he began to develop some of the symptoms that tend to accompany aging. He was well beyond the time of life when as a young priest, and then as a bishop and cardinal, he could spend days on end camping with young people, dedicating himself to outdoor pursuits such as swimming, skiing, or canoeing. In a physical sense, the pope grew old before his time, worn down by the difficult years of his youth; by uncommon burdens, discomforts, and privations; and by the challenging ministry he carried out first in Poland and then as pope.

The year 1992 was marked by a serious medical operation carried out at Gemelli Hospital by Doctor Crucitti on July 15. This procedure was for the removal of a benign tumor on the colon. It was a tubulovillous adenoma with only one small site of high-grade dysplasia [a possible precursor to cancer]. The pope announced his impending hospitalization personally from the window of his apartment during his meeting with the faithful for the Sunday Angelus.

The pope's condition was relatively unobtrusive and did not give rise to many symptoms, and it had seemed so unimportant to him that he did not mention it for several months. As soon as he confided in me about the trouble he was experiencing, I immediately gave him verbal and written prescriptions for the appropriate examinations to be made, explaining what the likely diagnostic outcomes were. But the complete tests could not be administered until the beginning of July, according to a schedule determined by the Holy Father himself.

This operation also involved a long recovery time, but the Holy Father patiently endured it with his sights set on his trip to Santo Domingo in the Dominican Republic, for the 500-year anniversary of the evangelization of the Americas. It was his fifty-sixth international voyage outside of Italy.

John Paul II made 104 international voyages, the last one being to Lourdes, France, on August 14 and 15, 2004. He also made 146 visits to different parts of Italy, his last being to Loreto on September 5, 2004. Both of these were made in conjunction with feasts of the Blessed Virgin Mary. They were also very tiring for the pope, who was by then confined to a chair mounted on wheels. His voice had become feeble and faltering, his facial expression was frozen into a mask of suffering, and his gaze was already directed toward the distance ahead of him.

Even during previous visits, he had experienced health problems that were more or less serious. The pope confronted them with a steadfast will, and they were resolved through medical procedures that were sometimes quite daring, administered with the conviction that a pope's physical condition sometimes calls for measures unlike the more cautious ones used with ordinary people.

But Gemelli Hospital would once again merit the title of "Vatican III," which the pope had conferred upon it during an earlier recovery. Late in the morning of November 11, 1993, at the end of an audience in the Hall of Blessings, the Holy Father, descending from the platform, caught the hem of his vestment under the heel of his right shoe and fell heavily to the floor.

Doctor Gianfranco Fineschi, Director of the Institute of Clinical Orthopedics at Catholic University, administered general anesthesia to the pope, stemmed the bleeding in the traumatic lesion behind his right shoulder, and repositioned the Holy Father's dislocated arm, applying a cast.

As the pope's doctor, I was in a position to conjecture that some role had been played in this incident by a certain unsteadiness due to a neurological disturbance in the motor cortex of the brain, the first signs of which had been observed toward the end of 1991.

Parkinson's disease had begun to manifest itself with an occasional tremor in the fingers of the pope's left hand, and it had slowly progressed until he displayed all of the symptoms and impairments characteristic of the disease. Pharmaceutical treatment and physical therapy did not bring especially good results. Over the years, numerous medical consultants confirmed both the diagnosis and the therapeutic strategy.

The pope suffered another more serious fall on the evening of April 28, 1994. He slipped and fell in his apartment, fracturing and dislocating his right hip. In order to convince the pope of the seriousness of his injury, in addition to a visit from an orthopedic specialist, an X-ray was taken in the middle of the night. The pope had been scheduled to leave for a pastoral visit to Sicily the following day.

The hip replacement surgery was conducted by Doctor Fineshi at the Gemelli. This was followed by a lengthy recovery period and a difficult phase of physical and motor rehabilitation. The pope began using a cane almost everywhere he went. The coming years would see the use of a mobile platform by this ailing man less and less in command of his balance and movement.

On Christmas morning of 1995, televisions all over the world displayed a visibly suffering pope who read the traditional Christmas message from the window of his study and not from the balcony overlooking St. Peter's Square, as is the custom. The Holy Father unexpectedly interrupted the reading of Christmas greetings in various languages on account of an uncontrollable spasm, saying, "Excuse me, I need to stop." He immediately imparted a quick blessing and withdrew from the window, to the shock of the many thousands of people gathered in St. Peter's Square.

He did not come down for the 10:00 A.M. celebration of the third Christmas Mass, and the Holy See press office reported that the Holy Father was experiencing "a slight fever."

In reality, the pope had come down with an intestinal disorder accompanied by a fever, which would later show some improvement but with occasional flare-ups.

In light of the symptoms and of the negative results of a routine colonoscopy carried out at the beginning of December, that same day I made the diagnosis of acute appendicitis. This diagnosis was confirmed by a CAT scan taken on August 14, 1996, at Regina Apostolorum Hospital in Albano Laziale, after the pope suffered a relapse.

Unfortunately, the pope's many responsibilities, his understandable reluctance to undergo another operation, and the effectiveness of the non-surgical therapy that was administered all resulted in continual postponements of a new procedure.

John Paul's recurring health problems caused some public concern, and it was necessary to release a long explanation on September 14, which I wrote and signed and which was approved by the Holy Father after a medical consultation held two days earlier.

On October 8, John Paul II returned for the sixth time to an operating room in Gemelli Hospital, where Doctor Crucitti carried out the long-delayed intervention. The procedure confirmed the diagnosis of "recurring inflammations of the appendix."

To complicate the Holy Father's public and private life, in 2002 and 2003 he developed severe recurring pain in his right knee, due to advanced osteoarthritis. The most appropriate modern therapies were undertaken, while the pope rejected outright the surgical solution of a knee replacement.

What was the Holy Father's relationship with his physician like? Here is one of my personal recollections.

In July of 2004, during the pope's last summer vacation in Valle d'Aosta at Prat Sec near Courmayeur, on a rich green lawn beneath a blazing sun, I spoke with papal secretary Dziwisz (just one of many such occasions) about my proposal to resign after twenty-six years of service, it seeming reasonable to me that a replacement should be made. He told me that I could not and must not resign, because I was the Holy Father's own choice—the pope had, in fact, expressed this to me many times—and even revealed to me that the pope remembered his physician every day during Mass. It was a blackmail of sorts, and I had to give in.

On the other hand, I was aware of the Holy
Father's affectionate good will toward me. There had
been many modest displays of this over the years,
even including his desire to baptize my first niece, to
whom he gave the Polish nickname Olenka.

In the course of our professional and personal
relationship, which involved the treatment of everything from mild health problems to the acute and
chronic pathologies that affected his life and his pastoral and apostolic mission, John Paul II and I always
had a calm and direct way of communicating with
one another. He would ask me for concise but
detailed explanations, without yielding to an understandable curiosity about the smallest particulars or
asking for guaranteed prognoses.

He was very attentive to the symptoms he noticed
and described them very exactly, with the obvious
aim of enlightening the doctor and accelerating his
healing so he could return to work.

He always displayed an attitude of profound interior serenity, which—despite the occasional moment
of visible human disappointment and impatience—
led him to accept illness, pain, and forced inactivity
from the hands of God.

For these reasons, the doctor-patient relationship—marked by unhesitating trust on one side and
by respectful and prudent sincerity on the other—

saw very few moments of difficulty. The most trying times involved the serious medical decisions directly involving the Holy Father's health and apostolic ministry. But when it was necessary, the pope was the first to identify the most pressing needs and make the correct decision. And if there were delays or omissions on some occasions, these were choices that were made deliberately.

Beyond this, professional confidentiality and privacy still limit to some extent the narration of these experiences and recollections.

There are many other physicians, Italian and non-Italian, who have had the opportunity to use their expertise in the service of John Paul II. These doctors all had great experience, competence, and scientific prestige, some of them among worldwide leaders in their field. They included Catholics, Protestants, and Jews, and originated from Italy, Spain, Switzerland, Germany, France, the United Kingdom, the United States, and Poland. They all approached the pope with great devotion and carried out their work with delicate simplicity and great competence. And all of the consultants, with the exception of a few of my Italian colleagues, preserved a strict silence that bore witness to an admirable sense of professional discretion.

The hurried passing of the years continued to bring complications of the various pathologies that put the Holy Father's health to a difficult test. His medical care, involving many individual specialties, became increasingly more demanding, and his medical team, which discreetly followed the pope each time he left his private apartment, was in a constant state of tension and alarm.

On Sunday, January 30, 2005, the Holy Father recited the Angelus in raspy tones produced with great effort and visible suffering.

On January 31, the Holy See press office stated that the audiences scheduled for that day would be cancelled because the Holy Father was suffering from the flu, and later announced the resumption of the scheduled appointments and the cancellation of the general audience on Wednesday, February 2. In reality, his symptoms were relatively mild and gave no indication of a very rapid or serious development of dangerous complications.

And then began the most painful chapter of the complex medical issues that had marked the pontificate of John Paul II.

The Holy Father's precarious and fragile state of health was complicated by an acute inflammation of the larynx, with severe spasms that dangerously reduced his breathing capacity. On the evening of February 1, his condition worsened severely in just a few hours, and he developed a dangerous shortness of breath that made it necessary for him to be brought—in an ambulance equipped with life-support equipment—to Gemelli Hospital, where he arrived at 10:50 P.M. The Holy Father was brought to the room reserved for him on the tenth floor of the hospital.

There he was immediately administered the necessary respiratory assistance and diagnostic work.

He made good progress, and on Saturday, February 5, the Holy Father was able to watch peacefully in his room the television broadcast of the ceremony conducted in the Paul VI audience hall for Our Lady of Good Hope, patroness of the major seminary of Rome. His breathing had become regular enough again, and his general health was improving.

His stay at the hospital was prolonged for a few days in order to verify the stability of his condition. The pope concelebrated Holy Mass in his room each day. On Wednesday, February 9, the first day of Lent, the pope concelebrated the Eucharist and blessed the ashes that were administered to him by his personal secretary.

After the completion of the diagnostic tests—which included a total body CAT scan that permitted ruling out other pathologies, including tumors—on February 10 the pope returned by car to the Vatican at around 7:40 P.M. Before leaving the hospital, he gave the doctors personally signed copies of his recently published book, *Memory and Identity*. In an unusual gesture, he also gave extraordinary letters of praise and thanks to Doctor Lorenzo Ornagi, Rector of Catholic University, and to me in my capacity as Director of Health and Hygiene for Vatican City-State.

Over the following days the pope again developed recurring episodes of shortness of breath, which were closely monitored by the medical personnel of the Vatican responsible for his regular care. His condition was characterized by acute breathing difficulties caused by a preexisting and well-documented constriction of the larynx. The pope especially suffered from crises of labored breathing that affected the intake of breath and were often accompanied by the pathological obstruction of the breathing passages above the collarbone and of the spaces between the ribs.

It should be mentioned that during February and March, while the pope was at the Vatican, he underwent five video examinations of his larynx. These were conducted by Doctor Angelo Camaioni, the chief ear, nose, and throat specialist at San Giovanni Hospital in Rome, and one of the directors of health and hygiene for Vatican City-State.

Another crisis, approaching the point of asphyxiation, took place on the evening of February 23. During these frantic hours, Cardinal Marian Jaworski, the

Latin archbishop of Lviv, administered the sacrament of the Anointing of the Sick to his old friend. Although the pope's condition was adequately stabilized during the night, it was thought best to bring him to Gemelli Hospital. He was taken there shortly before noon on February 2.

It had become urgent to carry out a preventive tracheotomy with the permanent placement of an airway. The operation would make the pope's breathing more stable, but it would probably diminish his ability to form sounds.

With Doctor Rodolfo Proietti, Director of the Department of Admissions and Emergencies at Gemelli Hospital, I explained to the Holy Father the reasons for the operation, which was intended to guarantee him adequate respiration and avoid the crises of suffocation that had been his painful experience. The patient gave his consent, but not without asking with disarming simplicity whether it were possible to wait until after his summer vacation.

During the evening of that same day, the brief operation was carried out by Doctor Gaetano Paludetti, an orthodontist at Catholic University, and by Doctor Angelo Camaioni. Doctor Proietti oversaw the general anesthesia. Also present were myself and Doctor Enrico de Campora, an ear, nose, and throat specialist at the University of Florence, and a consultant for the Vatican's health and hygiene service.

After the operation, when the effects of the anesthesia had worn off and he had returned to his room, the pope asked for a piece of paper and wrote in Polish, with an unsteady hand, "See what they have done to me! But...*totus tuus!*"

It was an expression of amazement and distress at the sorry state to which he had been reduced, but one immediately elevated to an act of trust in Mary.

His postoperative recovery took place without complications, and he immediately began rehabilitation work for his breathing and speaking.

During these two periods of hospitalization, the Holy Father tried as much as possible to keep up with the lofty duties of his ministry, listening to letters that were read to him, signing documents, dictating texts, and meeting with his collaborators.

One authoritative witness of this is Pope Benedict XVI, who, in an interview aired on Polish television on October 17, 2005, recalled a visit with John Paul II at Gemelli Hospital in his capacity as Prefect of the Congregation for the Doctrine of the Faith. He described the visit, which took place around February 5 or 6, as follows:

> The pope suffered visibly, but he was fully conscious and very much present. I had simply gone for a working meeting, because I needed him to make a few decisions. In spite of his suffering, the Holy Father paid close attention to what I was saying. He

explained his decisions to me in a few words, gave
me his blessing, and addressed his parting words to
me in German, assuring me of his friendship and
trust.

On March 6, the Holy Father donned the traditional pink chasuble for Laetare Sunday (the fourth
Sunday during Lent) and celebrated Mass in the little chapel next to his hospital room. He was able to
make it all the way through to the final blessing, pronouncing this in a weak and trembling voice, but with
a certain degree of vocal control.

On Sunday, March 13, the pope returned to the
Vatican at around 6:40 P.M. As soon as he reached his
apartment, he went to the chapel to join in the
singing of the Lamentations of Jeremiah in Polish, a
commemoration of the Lord's passion.

Since February, there had been an efficient medical staff at the ready in the pope's apartment. In previous years, too, during critical phases of the pope's
health and after various surgical operations, I and my
colleagues had taken turns, night and day, in closely
monitoring the pope's condition. At times, this vigi-
lance had been extended for a number of weeks. The
oversight included the medical staff on duty around
the clock in Vatican City.

But the pope's difficult health conditions required
the installation of a more complex system. This team
included ten emergency care physicians and special-

ists in cardiology, infectious diseases, the respiratory system, internal medicine, radiology, and clinical pathology, assisted by four professional nurses, all under my direction. According to the peculiar and longstanding traditions of the pontifical medical staff and the Vatican health service, all of the doctors were drawn from a few of the prestigious public hospitals and two of the university faculties of the city of Rome. Like the humble Simon of Cyrene, we all assisted the elderly pope, our bishop, to carry his cross until the end. A full battery of modern equipment was always at the ready.

Over the following days the pope's general condition continued to improve, but this was impeded by his difficulty in swallowing and speaking, by a lack of proper nutrition, and by his significant physical weakness.

On Sunday, March 20, and Wednesday, March 23, the Holy Father appeared at the window of his study, unspeaking, limiting himself to imparting a blessing by simply making the sign of the cross with his right hand.

During Holy Week, the pope concelebrated the rites of the Easter Triduum in his private chapel, joining in the Stations of the Cross through a long and trying television linkup.

On March 27, Easter Sunday, the pope stood for almost thirteen minutes in front of his open window above St. Peter's Square, which was crowded with members of the faithful waiting for the Easter message. The pope held a copy of the address in his hands, while the Vatican's Secretary of State Cardinal Angelo Sodano read its contents, in a voice hoarse with emotion, from the balcony overlooking the square.

With admirable good will, the pope had at first tried to read the text aloud himself, and it seemed that his strenuous effort might allow him to succeed. But his attempt to pronounce the words of the ceremony failed, and with a sigh he whispered, "I can't speak" ; and then, in silence, he traced over the city and the world a large Sign of the Cross with his right hand. It was his last *Urbi et Orbi* blessing. These were the last days of the life of John Paul II, which Providence made coincide with the mystery of the passion, death, and resurrection of the Lord of glory.

On Easter Monday, the Holy Father did not appear at his study window.

On Wednesday, March 30, the Holy Father returned to the window and, without speaking, blessed the worried crowd waiting for him below in St. Peter's Square. It was the last public station of his own Way of the Cross.

On that same day, it was revealed that the pope was receiving nutrition through a permanent feeding tube, since eating had become too difficult.

On Thursday, March 31, a little after 11:00 A.M., the Holy Father, who had gone to his chapel to celebrate Mass, was seized by a violent fit of trembling. It was followed by a severe fever, with the pope's body temperature reaching 103.28 degrees. Then came a serious attack of septic shock and a cardiovascular collapse due to a urinary tract infection. The appropriate measures of cardiorespiratory treatment were immediately undertaken.

In response to a direct question from Archbishop Dziwisz, the pope clearly expressed his decision to remain in his apartment, where he was guaranteed specialized, uninterrupted, and expert medical assistance.

In the late afternoon, Mass was celebrated at the foot of the pope's bed. He concelebrated with his eyes closed, but at the moment of consecration he weakly raised his right arm twice, over the bread and the wine. He also made the gesture of striking his breast during the recitation of the *Agnus Dei*.

Cardinal Marian Jaworski administered the Sacrament of the Anointing of the Sick to him. At 7:17 P.M., the pope received Holy Communion.

At the end of the Mass, the pope's secretaries and the religious sisters of the papal household kissed his hand. The pope called each of them by name, adding "for the last time." The doctors and nurses, too, were emotionally moved as they approached. I clasped his hand firmly and said, "Your Holiness, we love you and we are close to you with all our heart."

Then the Holy Father asked to celebrate a Holy Hour of meditation and prayer, which was concluded with the sisters' singing.

On Friday, April 1, at 6:00 A.M., the pope, lucid and serene, put on a stole and pectoral cross and concelebrated the Mass.

At around 7:15, he followed the meditation of the fourteen Stations of the Cross with great recollection, making the Sign of the Cross at each station.

He then joined in the recitation of the third hour of the Divine Office and listened as the readings from Sacred Scripture were read by Father Tadeusz Styczen, his disciple.

The pope's medical condition had become extremely serious, characterized by an alarming compromise of his hematological and metabolic factors. His cardiovascular, respiratory, and renal systems were quickly failing.

John Paul could speak just a few words with great difficulty, but with an intense silence he participated in the constant prayer of those nearby him.

On the morning of Saturday, April 2, at 7:30 A.M., Mass was celebrated in the presence of the Holy Father.

He was beginning to flicker in and out of consciousness.

His temperature suddenly spiked late that morning. At around 3:30 P.M., in a very weak voice and with muffled words, the Holy Father asked in Polish to "let me go to the Lord."

For their part, the doctors realized that the end was near, and that any new aggressive therapeutic measures would be useless.

A little before 7:00 P.M., the Holy Father slipped into a coma. The monitor tracked the progressive failure of his vital functions.

In keeping with Polish tradition, a small lighted candle shone in the darkness of the room where the pope was expiring.

At 8:00 P.M., the celebration of the Mass for the feast of Divine Mercy was begun at the feet of the agonized Holy Father.

The presider of the ceremony was His Excellency Archbishop Stanislaw Dziwisz. Also participating were Cardinal Marian Jaworski, Archbishop Stanislaw Rylko, and Monsignor Mieczyslaw Mokrzycki. The religious sisters of the papal household, some priests and friends, and the doctors and nurses were gathered around the altar.

Polish religious songs accompanied the celebration, mingling with the songs of the young people and the multitude of the faithful gathered in St. Peter's Square.

The Holy Father passed away at 9:37 P.M.

Those present sang the *Te Deum* over his lifeless body. This hymn of praise and thanksgiving blended with the unanimous prayers that the Christian people gathered in the square directed toward the suddenly illuminated window of the pope's room.

The death, which I certified, was also verified by an electrocardiogram that lasted twenty minutes, according to Vatican norms.

For John Paul II, the "joyful hope"[35] had been fulfilled.

---

35. Cf. Prayer of the Mass during the Rite of Communion: "Deliver us, Lord, from every evil, and grant us peace in our day. In your mercy keep us free from sin and protect us from all anxiety as we wait in joyful hope for the coming of our Savior, Jesus Christ."

SAINTHOOD NOW!

by Angelo Comastri

*President of the Office
for the Infrastructure of St. Peter's
and Vicar General of the Holy Father
for Vatican City*

The Unanimous and Immediate Acclaim of the People of God

I N HIS HOMILY FOR THE HOLY MASS celebrated on April 20, 2005, in the Sistine Chapel at the conclusion of the conclave, Benedict XVI expressed himself as follows:

> I seem to feel his [John Paul II's] strong hand clasping mine; I seem to see his smiling eyes and hear his words, at this moment addressed specifically to me, "Do not be afraid!"
>
> The death of the Holy Father John Paul II and the days that followed have been an extraordinary period of grace for the Church and for the whole world. Deep sorrow at his departure and the sense of

emptiness that it left in everyone have been tempered by the action of the Risen Christ, which was manifested during long days in the unanimous wave of faith, love, and spiritual solidarity that culminated in his solemn funeral Mass.

We can say it: John Paul II's funeral was a truly extraordinary experience in which, in a certain way, we glimpsed the power of God who, through his Church, wants to make a great family of all the peoples by means of the unifying power of Truth and Love (cf. *Lumen Gentium,* no. 1). Conformed to his Master and Lord, John Paul II crowned his long and fruitful pontificate at the hour of his death, strengthening Christian people in their faith, gathering them around him, and making the entire human family feel more closely united.

These words from Benedict XVI express the feelings that we all experienced—and continue to experience, by participating in the continual and devoted pilgrimage of the crowds before the tomb of the deceased pontiff. The popular weekly Italian magazine *Famiglia Cristiana,* in a survey of its readers conducted a few days after the death of the pope, gathered a great number of testimonies that strike the heart with their immediacy, their clarity, and the diversity of their origins. Here are just a few of the most beautiful of these calls for the proclamation of his sanctity:

———◆———

"I want him to be declared a saint because he succeeded in guiding us into the third millennium by taking the heart of the world into his hands with certainty and courage, as Christ did." *(Italy)*

———◆———

"...Because he was a great Father of the Church, a heroic and tireless witness of the Word of God, which he brought to every corner of the world. He showed great steadfastness in the faith and in carrying out the will of God until the last moment of his life." *(Italy)*

———◆———

"I would like him to be proclaimed a saint because, for me, the pope was the Gospel come to life and lived heroically." *(Lebanon)*

———◆———

"...Because he changed history, he was like a father and a mother, too; he gave us the true life of Jesus." *(Czech Republic)*

—◆—

"For his tireless work on behalf of the unity of all Christians." *(Croatia)*

—◆—

"I still treasure in my heart the way the pope looked at me, full of love, when he came to my beloved country, and this has always pulled me forward in the most difficult moments of my apostolate." *(Pakistan)*

—◆—

"I want him to be declared a saint because he was a true image of Jesus on earth." *(Israel)*

—◆—

"...Because he loved without waiting to be loved first and without expecting anything in return." *(Portugal)*

—◆—

"Pope Wojtyla revealed to us, through his life, the tenderness of the Father, the love of Christ, and the beauty of Mary." *(China)*

"I would like him to be declared a saint because he impacted the history of my country at a time when human rights were being trampled down, and because he spoke out on behalf of the weakest." *(Chile)*

"...Because he was a man of deep prayer, and he loved everyone, especially the smallest and the poorest, and he never failed to speak out against war, always listening to the Holy Spirit." *(Great Britain)*

"...Because he knew how to recognize the signs of the times, and he brought God close to all, wherever they are: work, family, social life." *(Switzerland)*

"For me, making him a saint would be a way of telling him 'thank you' and paying back the love that he gave to all of us." *(Malta)*

Father Raymond Zambelli, rector of the sanctuary of Notre Dame of Lourdes, released this statement a few days after the pontiff's death: "When I was a child, I envied the persons who had, during their life, the privilege of meeting a saint, of seeing him and watching him pray. Now I can say that we have received this grace. On August 15, 2004, we were visited by a saint at Lourdes! We saw with our own eyes a person who had been shaped entirely by the Beatitudes, and he affected us deeply. We were all impacted by his total abandonment in the arms of God; by his humility and his patience in trials; by his courage, his profound recollection, his interiority, goodness, sweetness, and his wonderful closeness to the sick and the lowly. And what can one say about his immense love for the Holy Eucharist and his great tenderness toward the Immaculate?"

So no one was surprised when the Holy Father Benedict XVI made public the decision to give immediate approval for the cause of John Paul II's beatification.

Here is the text of the declaration issued by the Congregation for the Causes of Saints, signed by Cardinal José Saraiva Martins and by the congregation's secretary, His Excellency Archbishop Edward Nowak: "At the request of the Most Eminent and Reverend Lord Cardinal Camillo Ruini, Vicar General of His Holiness for the Diocese of Rome, the Supreme Pontiff Benedict XVI, having considered the particular circumstances explained by the Cardinal Vicar during the audience granted to him on the 28th of the month of April of this year of 2005, granted a dispensation from the waiting period of five years after the death of the Servant of God John Paul II, such that the cause of Beatification and Canonization of this Servant of God may begin immediately. Given in Rome, from the office of this Congregation for the Causes of Saints, May 9, 2005."

And so, in the month of May, Mary's month, there began the journey toward the honor of the altar...of a man who described himself as "entirely Mary's": *Totus tuus!*

Some Personal Recollections

On April 1, 2005, the evening before the pious death of John Paul II, I was in my office near St. Peter's Basilica. The telephone rang. I picked up the receiver and immediately recognized the voice of His Excellency Archbishop Stanislaw Dziwisz, the Holy Father's personal secretary. He told me, "The pope is dying. If you would like, come say goodbye to him and receive a last blessing." Seized by emotion, I ran toward the pope's apartment. Archbishop Dziwisz was waiting for me at the door, and he brought me into the pope's private chamber. I saw the pope breathing with great difficulty, assisted by a doctor who was administering oxygen to him. His hands were bloated, and he seemed ready to throw off his chains and begin the great journey; his eyes were serene, as if he were already looking beyond this world to glimpse the Holy Face, the Face he longed for, the beloved Face of him who had been the entire reason of his life.

I burst into tears and knelt at the pope's bedside, and there suddenly came back to my mind's eye a scene from the previous Good Friday: the television screen had shown the pope seated in his private chapel, holding the crucifix in his hands; the crucifix was not turned outward, however, but toward the pope himself, who was gazing at it as he entered into the agony of his Divine Master.

At that moment, in the interior silence of my soul, I felt the words that Jesus addressed to Simon Peter on the shore of the Sea of Galilee: "'Simon, son of John, do you love me more than these?' He said to him, 'Yes, Lord; you know that I love you.' Jesus said to him, 'Feed my lambs.... Very truly, I tell you, when you were younger, you used to fasten your own belt and to go wherever you wished; but when you grow old, you will stretch out your hands, and someone else will fasten a belt around you and take you where you do not wish to go.' (He said this to indicate the kind of death by which he would glorify God.) After this he said to him, 'Follow me'" (Jn 21:15, 18–19).

While I knelt beside the bed of the dying pope, it seemed to me that he was living this passage from the Gospel, this perpetual dialogue between the Lord and Peter; and on the lips of the pontiff I perceived the astonishing summary of his life and his long and dramatic pontificate: "Lord, you know everything. You know that I love you" (Jn 21:17).

———◆———

The evening of that day, St. Peter's Square was spontaneously filled with a dense, enormous crowd of people: we prayed the holy Rosary together in subdued voices and with visible emotion, while the lighted windows of the pope's chamber seemed like two eyes that watched us, caressed us, and blessed us, imparting to us the message of the beginning and end of this pontificate: "Be not afraid! Open; indeed, throw open wide the doors for Christ!"

Almost by an impulse, I said into the microphone, "Now there is a special significance for the words that John Paul II pronounced in this square at the beginning of his pontificate, on October 16 of 1978: at this moment, Christ is throwing wide open the doors of paradise, while Mary stands waiting, smiling at the door to embrace him and welcome him to the feast of the saints."

We know what happened on that day and during the days that followed; this now belongs to history and to the storehouse of our memories.

I will recount just two episodes that I witnessed personally.

When the pontiff's venerable body was brought into the Vatican basilica, a worldwide pilgrimage began that seemed like an embrace of affection and regard for the man who had walked so tirelessly as a pilgrim of the Gospel down the roads of the entire world. During the first night, while the crowd was silently and slowly passing before the pope, I heard a man call out to me who had come up to the barrier between the crowd and the coffin. He said, "Father, I must kneel before the pope! Help me, get me through! I'm begging you!" Gently but firmly, I replied, "Try to understand! There are so many people. It's not possible. You must be satisfied with just walking past." The man insisted, grasped my hand, and, almost weeping, repeated, "I must kneel before the pope. I must thank him. I had lost my faith and had completely left the Church. The faith of that man," and here he pointed to the pope, "brought me back to the faith." I let him through, and he knelt in prayer. I stood close behind him, and suddenly noticed that he was weeping, seized by uncontrollable emotion. Then he stood and moved away. I have no idea who he was—I'll find out in heaven.

Two days later, the pilgrimage was still going on. The flood of visitors seemed even to have grown in size and intensity. One young man in his early twenties made a sign that he wanted to speak with me. I was hesitant to approach him, because I was afraid that he, too, wanted an exception from the procedures necessary for order. But he was so insistent that I had to go hear what he had to say. When I had reached him, he rolled up his sleeve, exposing his whole right arm, and I saw the unmistakable signs of repeated drug injections. The young man whispered to me, weeping, "I am old, but that old man was young! I'm not asking to get closer. Just kiss his feet for me: that will be my thanks!" With tears in my eyes, I carried out the mission entrusted to me by that unknown young man: I kissed the pope's feet, and said "thank you."

Messages Left on the Pope's Tomb

While, amid a general atmosphere of shock, the silent and devout pilgrimage continued before the simple and luminous tomb of John Paul II, every day many little notes were left there, like flower petals. In them, the visitors opened their hearts and offered to the pope their sorrows, hope, or some personal concern.

With care and diligence I selected some of the messages, and the first impression that I drew from them was that the people were asking for the intercession of John Paul II because they considered him a saint. They invoked him above all as the patron of young people and of the family, and of those who ask for the strength to forgive or to bear sickness or other sufferings.

As if paging through a family album or a book of prayers, I note some of the thoughts expressed for the benefit of all:

———◆———

"I would like to learn to forgive as you did." *(These words were written beneath a little drawing placed together with others by an Italian schoolgirl.)*

———◆———

"I implore you: help all mothers to give love and attention to all of the children the Lord gives them." *(A mother)*

———◆———

"Guide all young people who no longer believe in love and who pursue fleeting passions without giving value and meaning to their acts, which are devoid of authentic love." *(A young person)*

———◆———

"I thank you for bringing me to conversion." *(A father)*

———◆———

"For my son and my husband, that they may continue along the Christian way: this is the most important thing in life." *(A wife)*

———◆———

"I see the world and my life through new eyes. I have discovered that I must learn to accept life's problems as Jesus carried his cross: without hatred, without anger, but with love and maturity...as John Paul II carried us! The Kingdom of God unquestionably exists: he showed us this...and this is no longer a mystery for me. Thank you, Pope John Paul II!" *(A young man)*

———◆———

"Help me to live out my love in purity and truth."
(A young man)

———◆———

"Make me good, Holy Father! Give me a bit of
the joy that I desire so much. Bless my soul: you know
who I am and what I want, because you are a saint."
(Anonymous)

———◆———

"Among the many words you spoke to us, I was
struck by the ones you said in St. Peter's Square at the
beginning of the Jubilee for Young People. You asked
us emphatically, 'Whom do you seek?' In just a few
words you invited us to clarify our doubts and uncer-
tainties." *(A young man)*

———◆———

"John Paul, I write to you to ask you for something, something big. I was never close to the Church;
it bored me, and I didn't understand it. Love, yes—
that I have always understood! And it is out of pure
love that I write to you, for the love of my grandmother. I deserve nothing; I have always been far
[from the Church]...but she deserves it! I always trust-

ed you—you were different, you *really* loved. One could not—one cannot—help but love you, and seek out your expression full of love and compassion for all. Save my grandmother, and bring me close to God!" *(A young woman)*

"Help me through this difficult moment in my life! Help me to suffer with dignity and patience...as you did. I beg you: heal me! Or help me to recover my health enough that I can take care of my family. Protect and guide my children.... I will always keep in my heart your words: 'Be not afraid.'" *(A mother)*

"Bring to our heavenly Mother our appeal as parents! [Bring her] the decisions we must make, our hopes, our desires for the good of our children." *(A father and mother)*

"I ask you to intercede for the purification the Church! May the Holy Spirit embrace all bishops and priests!" *(Unsigned)*

—◆—

"On Thursday afternoon, I spent an hour in prayer at my parish, and a photo of you had been placed next to the altar. I turned toward it and said, 'Now you are close to God! Do me the favor of finding a job for my son, who has been seeking one for a long time.' The next day, on Friday, my son told me that he had found a job, a good job! Thank you!" *(A mother)*

—◆—

"Dear Pope, in twenty-four hours I will be taking my graduation exams, and I'm scared. I am sure I will have your help...because I think you're too good not to think about me, too! And just in case you have a little extra time, turn toward me and brush away this dark speck of trouble that's buzzing around me. When you went away, there were tears in every eye: you were truly a great man! Perhaps I discovered this too late! I love you." *(A young student)*

—◆—

"Beloved Pope John Paul II, I believe that you, looking down from heaven upon the many children suffering on earth...will bring their tears to the Father and do all you can to help them! Help me to become holy...like you did!" *(Signed, "from Nigeria")*

—◆—

"I ask you for the grace of my ongoing conversion! May my heart burn always with the only love worth living for: that of Jesus Christ!" *(A priest)*

—◆—

"Dear Pope John Paul II, thank you for loving us so much! Your silent blessing, in these noisy times ...was a prophetic gesture of amazing power. You brought me closer to God! Forgive me for the time when I did not understand you!" *(A young woman)*

—◆—

"Dear Karol, I love you, I venerate you, and I entrust myself to your powerful intercession. You lost your mother a few years after you were born, and I lost mine when I was eighteen. Then I was called to war. I, too, was born in 1920. You adopted all of humanity, and my wife and I adopted a girl many years ago. Before long, we will meet together in

Christ. Meanwhile, I entrust to you my adopted daughter...my son-in-law, and my nephews, that they may all increase in goodness, hope, and charity." *(A grandfather)*

———◆———

And finally, a girl in the fifth grade left on the pope's tomb this exquisitely simple and beautiful poem:

> Beloved pope who was so dear,
> You have gone away—
> but where?
> To go and teach the Gospel way
> That makes all people family!
> You traveled over all the earth
> And opened minds as went you forth;
> You visited the sick, and gave
> The strength they needed to be brave;
> You walked the prisons and wept for all
> The sins of every criminal.
> You went to the young...
> To Paul and John...
> And made them friends so very soon![36]

---

36. Loose poetic translation.

The Last Note Left on the Tomb of John Paul II

I would like the last note on the pope's tomb to be brought by...me! But it is not my own prayer, even though I share it and make it my own, acknowledging it as the heartfelt expression of my heart as a Christian and a bishop.

I will explain. On Good Friday, March 25, 2005, during the spiritually moving Way of the Cross held every year at the Colosseum, at the ninth station there was a courageous proclamation that I still keep in the sanctuary of my conscience:

> Lord, your Church often seems like a boat about to sink, a boat taking in water on every side. In your field we see more weeds than wheat. The soiled garments and face of your Church throw us into confusion. Yet it is we ourselves who have soiled them! It is we who betray you time and time again, after all our lofty words and grand gestures. Have mercy on your Church; within her, too, Adam continues to fall. When we fall, we drag you down to earth, and Satan laughs, for he hopes that you will not be able to rise from that fall; he hopes that being dragged down in the fall of your Church, you will remain prostrate and overpowered. But you will rise again. You stood up, you arose, and you can also raise us up. Save and sanctify your Church. Save and sanctify us all.[37]

---

37. Cardinal Joseph Ratzinger, *Way of the Cross* (Boston: Pauline Books & Media, 2005), pp. 87–88.

These words were written by then-Cardinal Joseph Ratzinger, now Benedict XVI. I would like to give them over to John Paul II, that he may uphold them with the power of his prayer and intercession before God, inspiring Benedict XVI to take the steps and make the decisions necessary to cleanse "the garments and face" of the Church, that the beautiful face of Jesus may shine forth from it.

And I find the response to this in the moving words pronounced by the Holy Father Benedict XVI at the end of the homily at the funeral Mass for John Paul II: "We can be sure that our beloved pope is standing today at the window of the Father's house, that he sees us and blesses us. Yes, bless us, Holy Father. We entrust your dear soul to the Mother of God, your Mother, who guided you each day and who will guide you now to the eternal glory of her Son, our Lord Jesus Christ. Amen."[38]

Identifying Some of the Main Themes of John Paul II's Sanctity

I certainly don't want to anticipate the judgment that is for the Church, and the Church alone, to make. I will simply make a few suggestions that seem to emerge straight off from observation and reflection on the life of John Paul II.

---

38. Official Vatican translation from www.vatican.va.

One consideration comes first. With the passing of time, many persons, including so-called "celebrities," are forgotten. If you want, try stopping one day in front of the Palatine ruins (the exquisite ancient imperial palace) in Rome: here lived men who had themselves called "divine"; men who shook the world, who moved armies and displaced peoples with a mere gesture (for example, think of the census called by Caesar Augustus at the time of Jesus: this census put the whole Empire into motion!). Today the Palatine is nothing but a ruin overrun with the silence of history and human disregard.

But something unusual is happening with John Paul II: as the days and months pass slowly by, his memory is growing, affection is growing, admiration and gratitude for him are growing. The streets and squares being dedicated to him are innumerable, while historians and archivists struggle to compile even an incomplete and temporary assessment of his life. And the procession of the crowds continues, faithful and devout, before his humble tomb carved into the earth of the Vatican hill, like that of Paul VI and that of the first pope, Peter. What is happening here is undeniable.

But is it possible to outline John Paul II's sanctity?

It seems to me that John Paul II should be recognized for one virtue that is not at all insignificant: *he was a man of courage at a time of great fear;* he was a decisive and consistent man in an era of compromise, chronic uncertainty, and widespread unsteadiness. He exemplified wonderfully these words of Jesus:

> "What I say to you in the dark, tell in the light; and what you hear whispered, proclaim from the housetops. Do not fear those who kill the body but cannot kill the soul; rather fear the one who can destroy both soul and body in hell. Are not two sparrows sold for a penny? Yet not one of them will fall to the ground apart from your Father. And even the hairs of your head are all counted. So do not be afraid; you are of more value than many sparrows. Everyone therefore who acknowledges me before others, I also will acknowledge before my Father in heaven; but whoever denies me before others, I also will deny before my Father in heaven" (Mt 10:27–33).

———◆———

He was courageous in defending peace while winds of war were blowing. Who does not recall the repeated and anguished appeals he made, regardless of whether he would be heard? He sometimes seemed like a prophet speaking in a desert of indifference, yet John Paul II did not let himself be discouraged; he continued to speak as the Spirit of Jesus prompted him in the sanctuary of his conscience.

Who does not recall with emotion and admiration the cry he uttered on March 16, 2003, at the end of the spiritual retreat he made each year at the beginning of Lent? From the window of his apartment, he exclaimed fearlessly, "I know, I know what war is! It is my duty to tell those [who believe in war] that war increases hatred and does not resolve problems."

What courage! At that moment his way of speaking went against an overwhelming tide, but John Paul II risked unpopularity on a number of occasions in order to remain tenaciously loyal to his task as a servant of the truth, the truth that Jesus entrusted to the Church, and in particular to the one he nicknamed "Rock."

More than once, when I was listening to the words of John Paul II, there came to mind this dazzling assertion from the Apostle Paul: "For we cannot do anything against the truth, but only for the truth" (2 Cor 13:8). I also applied to the pontificate of John Paul II what the Apostle of the Gentiles said about the difficulties of his ministry. "...on frequent journeys, in danger from rivers, danger from bandits, danger from my own people, danger from Gentiles, danger in the city, danger in the wilderness, danger at sea, danger from false brothers and sisters; in toil and hardship, through many a sleepless night, hungry and thirsty, often without food, cold and naked. And, besides other things, I am under daily pressure because of my anxiety for all the churches. Who is weak, and I am not weak? Who is made to stumble, and I am not indignant?" (2 Cor 11:26–29)

———◆———

John Paul II was a man of courage in defending the family at a time that had lost the understanding of the irreplaceable husband/wife and father/mother duality. With a prophetic eye, Pope Wojtyla keenly perceived that what is at risk today is *the very humanity of man,* the intrinsic design of humanity as a family, as a man and woman who become, through faithful love, a cradle of life and an irreplaceable environment for the growth and development of human life.

I think that John Paul II felt deeply wounded in his heart when the news came out that the European Parliament had not been able to reach agreement on defining the family. This was an extremely serious matter, and it indicated the loss of Europe's self-awareness. Driven, perhaps, by this alarming fact, the pope launched himself like an athlete to the defense of the family. The World Days of the Family, the Jubilee of Families, the constant messages to married couples and families were the fruit of a steadfast love and, at the same time, a clever way of reeducating the peoples and governments of nations on the values that form an authentic civilization. If the family falls, what remains of society? If the family disappears, what beacon will guide children along the journey of life?

John Paul II understood all of this, and it prompted him to teach insistently and in depth on the value and meaning of the family. It may be that in a few years or decades we will be better able to appreciate the work John Paul II carried out to restore the meaning of the family amid the darkening of the modern mind.

He was a man of courage in defending the dignity of human life, of every human life: white, yellow, or black; healthy or infirm; rich or poor; from conception to death. The encyclical *Evangelium Vitae* is an extraordinary document, speaking to both mind and heart. John Paul II sought in every way possible to explain that the defense of life is not solely a religious principle, nor an interference of religion in the political sphere, but an argument of pure and coherent logic as the basis of civil coexistence. Besides, if the right to life is not guaranteed, what other right can still be guaranteed? John Paul II was particularly attentive to this topic, and his great soul was always on the alert whenever the defense of human life was at stake.

Who does not remember the sudden fury that shook the pope at Temple Valley near Agrigento?[39] In a voice worthy of Amos or Hosea, and in powerful terms like those of Isaiah, he shouted amid the general shock of those present, "Men of the Mafia, reform your lives! One day you will give an account before God of what you are doing now!" At that moment, everyone realized that the pope was exposing himself to the risk of vendetta[40] and, perhaps, of another attempt on his life. But John Paul II was prepared to sacrifice his life: during his pontificate he had often tread upon the asp and the viper,[41] trusting entirely in the help and protection of the Lord.

At the same time, John Paul II defended the inviolable and captivating mystery of all human life, reminding us that justifying an attack on human life at its birth or death opens the door to justifying any violence at any moment of human existence.

He understood well—and how often he recalled this in a voice full of anguish!—that the terrible violations of human life committed by the totalitarian regimes of the twentieth century stemmed from misconceptions about human nature; that is, they stemmed from errors about the value of the human person and came to the point of differentiating hu-

---

39. In Sicily, the Mafia's home turf.
40. The Mafia's various vicious forms of revenge.
41. Cf. Psalm 91:13.

man life, deciding in an arbitrary and diabolical fash-
ion who should live and who should die, who has
more dignity and who less. In this area, too, we will
eventually see how providential and farseeing the
activity of John Paul II was.

———◆———

*He was a man of courage in seeking out young people
and speaking to young people.* At the beginning of his
pontificate, it seemed that the Church was no longer
able to speak the language of youth and no longer
had credibility among the younger generations. John
Paul II refused to bury his head in the sand. He knew
that without Christ, young people would never be
able to find meaning in life and would never be able
to experience the captivating reality of love, which is
a gift of self rather than a whim that bends everything and everyone to one's own purposes. The pope
sought out the young, and the young recognized him
as their friend, an authentic and sincere friend who
did not sacrifice his principles for the sake of gaining
an audience, a friend who did not water down the
challenge of the Gospel in order to be popular, a
friend who did not use cheap rhetoric to win the
applause of the young.

And yet the young applauded him warmly, spontaneously, and with demonstrations of approval that

deflated those who had predicted the Church's demise and the extinction of Christianity.

The young loved John Paul II intensely, and they sought him out like a father who, when it is appropriate, knows also how to issue correction because he knows how to love truly and faithfully.

I get goose bumps when I think about how he welcomed the young people in St. Peter's Square at the beginning of World Youth Day, in the August heat of the year 2000! His words rang out suddenly in that robust voice: "Whom do you seek?" I remember that we bishops, too, were surprised and captivated by the power of this question. And the pope immediately exclaimed that he did not intend to lower the standards in order to win the young people over, but to courageously invite them to raise themselves up in order to give dignity and meaning to their lives.

In their turn, the youth understood that this elderly man knew the secret of their young lives, and they became attentive and thoughtful.

And on the evening of the long prayer vigil in the immense open field of Tor Vergata, something else happened that should not be forgotten, because it was a sign of the extraordinary relationship that had been established between the pope and young people. While the serene skies of Rome were filled with songs from the assembly of youth from five continents, a young man suddenly leapt past the security line, evaded the grasp of a burly policeman, and rushed up to the pope. The old man and the young man looked at each other for a moment, and then they embraced with the intensity with which a father embraces his own son. Emotion flooded the hearts of everyone there—and I wept!

———◆———

He was, finally, a man of courage in the difficult season of illness and at the moment of death.

During his illness, which gradually deprived John Paul II of his most brilliant and treasured personal qualities, he did not go into hiding. It must have cost him dearly, but he did not permit a veil to protect him from the indiscreet eyes of others: he lived his illness publicly, turning it into a living homily that touched the hearts of all humanity.

From many quarters came insistent and disrespectful calls for the pope's resignation, and I think this really wounded his heart.

John Paul II decided not to descend from the cross, however, but to spend himself to the last ounce of his strength. I can still see him on the last Wednesday of his life, coming to the window of his apartment. He tried several times to speak; he focused his strength on giving voice to the feelings in his heart, but no sound would come from his trembling lips. And yet that Wednesday was one of the most intense, profound, and touching moments of his long magisterium: by his eloquent silence, the pope told everyone that in order to be like Jesus, we must love until the very end, to the point of giving our entire lives for him who gave his life for us.

Where did the pope find this courage?

He found it in a faith nourished by continual prayer. They have told me that, during his repeated and tiring voyages all over the world, John Paul II rose in the morning before everyone else and prostrated himself in prayer before the tabernacle—and, like Moses, his face was suffused with light.

Cardinal Andrea Deskur, a friend of the pope's since their youth, told me that, needing to accommodate Cardinal Wojtyla during his frequent visits to Rome, he saw that he would have to change the flooring in the chapel. The future pope, in fact, was on a number of occasions found by his friend prostrate in prayer upon the cold floor. To avoid the possibility of irreversible harm to the indomitable devotee's health, he replaced the hard tiles with wood.

I CONCLUDE WITH A REQUISITE mention of John Paul II's Marian devotion. The years of 1965–1975 were a sort of Marian winter: it seemed that suddenly many, too many, were doing all they could to marginalize Mary in order (they said) to restore centrality to Jesus Christ. This argument was nothing but a pretense, because the Son and the Mother are not alternatives, but instead go together. And John Paul II restored Mary to her place in the Church next to Jesus. It is by beginning with Jesus, in fact, that one arrives at Mary; it is by beginning with Jesus that one discovers the presence of his Mother and her irreplaceable mission, which is not that of replacing her Son, but that of bringing us to him!

John Paul II had a sensitivity, an insight, an intuition all his own in relation to the presence and mission of Mary.

His episcopal and pontifical coat of arms proclaimed his devotion: the letter "M," which stood out on a blue background, was accompanied by the son's cry to his Mother: *Totus tuus*.

How beautiful all of this is: beautiful in human terms and beautiful in Christian terms!

Examining the actions and gestures of John Paul II, meditating on his speeches and documents, one realizes that his affection for Mary was a source of inspiration that characterized his journey in the footsteps of Jesus.

On June 4, 1979, as the pope was making the first-ever pontifical pilgrimage to Jasna Góra, he entrusted the Church to Mary, pronouncing emotional and touching words:

How many problems, O Mother, I should have presented to you at this meeting, listing them one by one. I entrust them all to you, because you know them better than we do and you take care of them all.

I do so in this hallowed place which embraces not only Poland, but all of the Church as it extends through countries and across continents, all of the Church, in your motherly heart. I offer you the whole Church, of which I am the first servant, and I entrust it to you with immense confidence, O Mother.

In his tireless journeying across the various continents, the pope always kept his eyes fixed upon Mary. It was from her that he learned and proclaimed the beauty of fidelity to the Lord and his Gospel; it was from her that he heard and then transmitted the hope of the Magnificat; it was from her that he learned to make Christ the center of all of his pastoral activity, because Mary constantly tells us, "Whatever Jesus tells you, do it!" (cf. Jn 2:5).

This brings clarity and poignancy to the pope's gesture when, after the dramatic attack on May 13, 1981, he went to Fatima to thank Mary, presenting to her the lethal bullet that had failed to kill him; it explains his constant pilgrimages to Marian shrines, where "it is as if we absorb the faith of Mary" (letter for the 700th anniversary of the shrine of Loreto); it illuminates the pope's reason for clutching the rosary tightly in his hands to feel the solidity and tenderness of his Mother; it clarifies the fidelity to the recitation of the Angelus that the pope brought to the streets, squares, and countrysides of the entire world.

I was in Fatima on May 13, 2000, and I still treasure in my heart the moment when the Holy Father John Paul II beatified the two shepherds of Fatima, Jacinta and Francisco, in the presence of the third shepherdess, Lucia, and in the presence of an enormous crowd of pilgrims who had come (many of them by foot) from all of Portugal and from the farthest corners of the earth.

How wonderfully real the Magnificat of Mary seemed to me just then! How palpable and immediate seemed that song of praise that is passed down from generation to generation!

In the immense open field of Cova da Iria, a sea of faces illuminated by the sun moved like a single wave kissed by the Spirit's divine breath: it was the people of the "lowly," to which Mary belonged and of which she spoke in the Magnificat; it was the people of the "humble," of those who slept in the open air because they could not afford the luxury of a hotel room. But at that moment, this people of the "humble" clearly felt that they were the fulfillment of Mary's words.

And emotion turned to surprise when, at the end of the beatification ceremony for the two shepherds,

Cardinal Angelo Sodano, secretary of state for His Holiness, spoke out in the name of the pope:

> As you know, the purpose of his visit to Fatima has been to beatify the two "little shepherds." Nevertheless he also wishes his pilgrimage to be a renewed gesture of gratitude to Our Lady for her protection during these years of his papacy. This protection seems also to be linked to the so-called "third part" of the secret of Fatima.
>
> That text contains a prophetic vision similar to those found in Sacred Scripture, which do not describe with photographic clarity the details of future events, but rather synthesize and condense against a unified background events spread out over time in a succession and a duration which are not specified. As a result, the text must be interpreted in a symbolic key.
>
> The vision of Fatima concerns above all the war waged by atheist systems against the Church and Christians, and it describes the immense suffering endured by the witnesses to the faith in the last century of the second millennium. It is an interminable Way of the Cross led by the popes of the twentieth century.
>
> According to the interpretation of the "little shepherds," which was also recently confirmed by Sister Lucia, the "Bishop clothed in white" who prays for all the faithful is the pope. As he makes his way with great effort toward the cross amid the corpses of those who were martyred (bishops, priests, men and women religious, and many lay

persons), he too falls to the ground, apparently dead, under a burst of gunfire.

After the assassination attempt of May 13, 1981, it appeared evident to His Holiness that it was "a motherly hand which guided the bullet's path," enabling the "dying Pope" to halt "at the threshold of death."[42] On the occasion of a visit to Rome by the then-bishop of Leiria-Fatima, the pope decided to give him the bullet which had remained in the jeep after the assassination attempt, so that it might be kept in the shrine. At the behest of the bishop, the bullet was later set in the crown of the statue of Our Lady of Fatima.

The successive events of 1989 led, both in the Soviet Union and in a number of countries of Eastern Europe, to the fall of the Communist regime which promoted atheism. For this too His Holiness offers heartfelt thanks to the Most Holy Virgin. In other parts of the world, however, attacks against the Church and against Christians, together with the burden of suffering which they involve, tragically continue. Even if the events to which the third part of the secret of Fatima refers now seem part of the past, our Lady's call to conversion and penance, issued at the beginning of the twentieth century, remains timely and urgent today. "The Lady of the message seems to read the signs of the times—the signs of our time—with special insight.... The insistent invitation of Mary Most

42. Pope John Paul II, Meditation with the Italian Bishops from the Policlinico Gemelli (*Insegnamenti*, vol. XVII/1, 1994, p. 1061).

Holy to penance is nothing but the manifestation of her maternal concern for the fate of the human family, in need of conversion and forgiveness."[43]

In order that the faithful may better receive the message of Our Lady of Fatima, the Pope has charged the Congregation for the Doctrine of the Faith with making public the third part of the secret, after the preparation of an appropriate commentary.[44]

At that moment, I had the clear perception that the events of Fatima were not the reason for the Marian devotion of John Paul II—it would be a serious error to think this, because the truth is the other way around. The Marian devotion of John Paul II, in fact, is the reason for and the explanation of the events of Fatima. Because the pope loved Mary and addressed to her his *Totus tuus*, she made him feel, through the events of Fatima, all of the truth and tenderness of her maternity.

So John Paul II's Marian devotion came before the connection between the attempt on his life and the message Mary gave to the shepherds, and was independent of Fatima. The pope's Marian devotion was entirely founded upon the Gospel, upon the Word of God. In the apostolic letter *Tertio Millennio*

---

43. Pope John Paul II, Message for the 1997 World Day of the Sick, no. 1 (*Insegnamenti*, vol. XIX/2, 1996, p. 561).

44. Official Vatican translation from www.vatican.va.

Adveniente, he wrote, "Mary's reply to the angel was unhesitating: 'Behold, I am the handmaid of the Lord; let it be to me according to your word' (Lk 1:38). Never in human history did so much depend, as it did then, upon the consent of one human creature."[45]

In this, too (in showing us the real and binding reason for Marian devotion), John Paul II was a faithful man, an authentic and courageous servant of the truth as revealed in the Gospels.

For this reason, our gratitude today is even stronger and more assured. And each time we grasp the holy rosary and recite the Hail Mary, a spontaneous acclamation bursts from our hearts: *Totus tuus,* Maria!

This is the Marian inheritance that John Paul II has left to us.

---

45. *Tertio Millennio Adveniente*, no. 2.

Pauline
BOOKS & MEDIA

The Daughters of St. Paul operate book and media centers at the following addresses. Visit, call or write the one nearest you today, or find us on the World Wide Web, www.pauline.org

CALIFORNIA
3908 Sepulveda Blvd, Culver City, CA 90230	310-397-8676
2640 Broadway Street, Redwood City, CA 94063	650-369-4230
5945 Balboa Avenue, San Diego, CA 92111	858-565-9181

FLORIDA
145 S.W. 107th Avenue, Miami, FL 33174	305-559-6715

HAWAII
1143 Bishop Street, Honolulu, HI 96813	808-521-2731
Neighbor Islands call:	866-521-2731

ILLINOIS
172 North Michigan Avenue, Chicago, IL 60601	312-346-4228

LOUISIANA
4403 Veterans Memorial Blvd, Metairie, LA 70006	504-887-7631

MASSACHUSETTS
885 Providence Hwy, Dedham, MA 02026	781-326-5385

MISSOURI
9804 Watson Road, St. Louis, MO 63126	314-965-3512

NEW JERSEY
561 U.S. Route 1, Wick Plaza, Edison, NJ 08817	732-572-1200

NEW YORK
150 East 52nd Street, New York, NY 10022	212-754-1110

PENNSYLVANIA
9171-A Roosevelt Blvd, Philadelphia, PA 19114	215-676-9494

SOUTH CAROLINA
243 King Street, Charleston, SC 29401	843-577-0175

TENNESSEE
4811 Poplar Avenue, Memphis, TN 38117	901-761-2987

TEXAS
114 Main Plaza, San Antonio, TX 78205	210-224-8101

VIRGINIA
1025 King Street, Alexandria, VA 22314	703-549-3806

CANADA
3022 Dufferin Street, Toronto, ON M6B 3T5	416-781-9131

¡También somos su fuente para libros,
videos y música en español!